# The Back Book

# THE BACK BOOK

# The Back Book

**Gavin Routledge and Gavin Hastings**

*in association with*

Makar Publishing

Originally published in 1999 by Thorsons
An Imprint of HarperCollins*Publishers*

This edition published by Makar Publishing in association with
Active$^{x}$ Osteopaths, 24 & 26 West Port, Edinburgh, EH1 2JE



ISBN 0-9551334-1-6

A catalogue record for this book is available from
the British Library



Photography by Robbie Smith
Illustrations by Peter Cox Associates

Design and production by
Makar Publishing Production, Edinburgh
Printed and bound in Great Britain by Lightning Source

To my wife Sandie,
for her continued love,
support and encouragement.

# Contents

# Acknowledgements

Thank you to all the patients who encouraged me to write this book. Thank you to all at Thorsons, particularly Nicky, Jo and Wanda for their support and expertise in producing the original edition, and for their permission and help to publish this new edition. Thanks also to Gillian Docking for her work on the manuscript and to all those who provided help and information in the compiling of this book.

# Foreword

The authors have something in common with the reader of this book – we have both suffered from a 'bad back'. The purpose of this book is to demonstrate that there is a way out for the 'bad back sufferer'. Through personal and clinical experience (and on the basis of scientific research) we have become convinced that the majority of sufferers can improve the state of their backs and decrease their pain levels. The way out that we present should not be viewed as the only one; however, *The Back Book* is the result of much research into low back pain – its causes, the treatments available, the most effective common solutions and the recommendations laid down by the Department of Health's Clinical Standards Advisory Group report into low back pain. Remember as you read this book that in so doing you are taking a DIY approach to caring for your back – while this is the point of the book, do not forget that there is a wealth of potential help for you out there in the form of experienced chiropractors, osteopaths and physiotherapists.

Whether you occasionally suffer a mild ache or are totally incapacitated by constant pain, this book will hold something for you – we guarantee it. Before you start reading, think about how long you have had a back problem. If it's only a week, you should prosper quickly from this book: if it's months or years, follow the advice in this book, but please allow several months for the benefit to show through. Between us we're trying to turn a poorly functioning back into a healthily functioning back; not just relieve the pain – if that was your sole aim, you could just go and buy some pain killers. Of course, sometimes they don't work!

The authors met when Gavin Hastings was 6 weeks away from an International rugby match against South Africa in 1994. He was suffering from acute low back pain – not for the first time – and Gavin Routledge was recommended to him.

Gavin Hastings OBE captained Scotland's International Rugby team 20 times and led the British Lions on their tour to New Zealand in 1993. Throughout his rugby career he has suffered episodes of acute low back pain. Although these episodes can result in great restriction of movement only a few have actually stopped him playing. However, he was frequently unable to sit for long periods due to the pain in his back; something he has in common with many bad back sufferers. A disc problem in his lower back was diagnosed, but this still did not stop him playing – he was as likely to suffer sitting on the team bus as on the pitch.

Gavin Routledge DO (Hons) is a registered osteopath practising in Edinburgh. He graduated in 1991 from the British School of Osteopathy, being awarded the gold medal for Conspicuous Merit on graduation. Since then he has worked in England, New Zealand and now Edinburgh. He has always maintained an interest in the potential role of exercise and posture in low back pain management. *The Back Book* is a collaborative effort between the two Gavins.

# How to Use this Book

**Are you suffering from acute back pain or chronic back pain?**

Acute pain:

- **Agonizing spasms of pain**
- **Lasting less than 6 weeks**
- **Severely limiting your ability to move around**

If two out of three of the above conditions apply to you, you are suffering from acute pain.

Chronic pain:

- **More than 6 weeks of pain on this occasion**
- **Recurrent episodes of pain**
- **Currently *not* severely limiting your ability to move around**

If two out of three of the above conditions apply to you, you are suffering from chronic pain.

- **If you are suffering acute pain start at 'Managing Acute Pain' page 1.**
- **If you are suffering chronic pain start at 'Understanding Back Pain' page 31.**
- **If you are normally in chronic pain but are suffering an acute episode then start at 'Managing Acute Pain' page 1.**

If you are using this book to recover from an episode of back pain you may feel you don't need to read the section entitled 'Understanding Back Pain'. However, the authors strongly recommend that you do, as it will help you to see how to avoid future recurrences of back pain and demystify back pain for you. Without understanding, how can you hope to prevent the same thing happening again?

Throughout this book you will come across the phrase **Use it or Lose it, but don't ever Abuse it**. This phrase sums up the whole essence of this book. If you do not use the physical capabilities you have, you will gradually lose them. In attempting to avoid pain by not doing certain things you will probably slowly stiffen up and lose the ability to do those things. So rest is not the answer – although it has a place. The answer lies in appropriate exercise and using the other strategies described in this book.

One very important thing to grasp about low back pain is that *no two back problems are the same*, because no two people are the same. So, when someone says to you, 'Oh yeah, I had exactly the same thing; it took 2 weeks to clear up,' DO NOT expect yours to do the same. And when they say 'You should try this exercise – it sorted mine out . . . ', remember what 'cures' one back problem can make another ten times worse. The advice given in this book is right for nearly all back problems (if your back does not improve consult a chiropractor, osteopath or physiotherapist – *see page 24*).

# Common Questions and Where to Find the Answers

# Managing Acute Pain

# Relaxation

**Don't worry** – nearly all back problems get better given time. The first step you need to take to ensure your back gets better is – **relax**! This may seem impossible to do when you're in agony, but it's vitally important that you learn.

- **Pain makes you tense.**
- **Tensing up makes the pain worse, and will slow down your recovery rate.**
- **Don't fight the pain – be calm.**
- **Painkilling drugs may help you to relax (*see page 147*).**
- **Muscle relaxants may help you to relax.**
- **If you need help, then ask!**

Find the most comfortable position to lie in. If it's still painful, try to focus in on that pain and do your best to let that whole area relax. Take a deep breath in, and as you breathe out – relax!

**When you lie down, make sure there is something next to you that you can grab hold of to help yourself up again.**

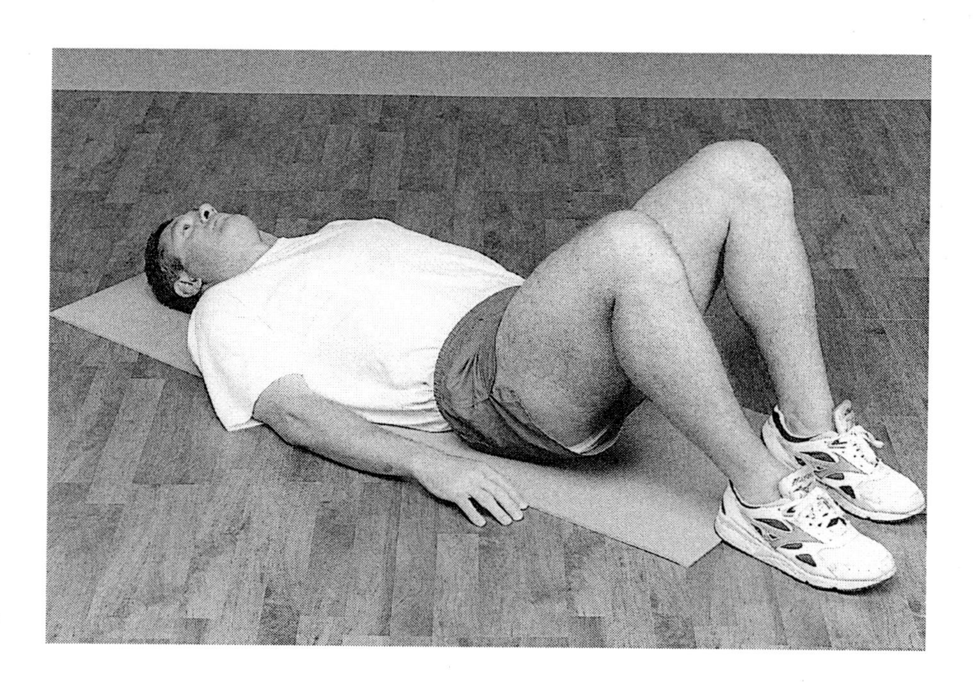

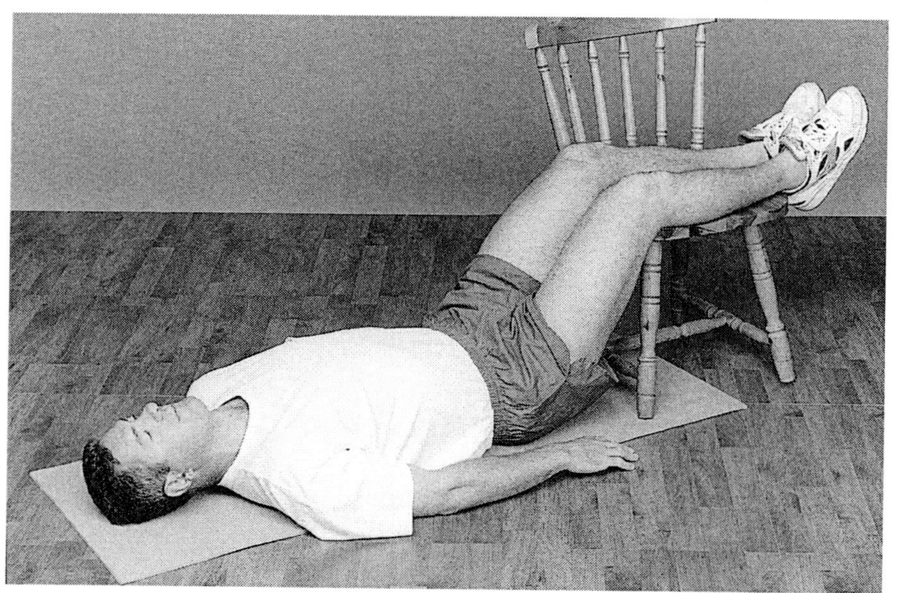

***Figure 1 Lying semi-supine***

Try to lie on your back with your head supported and your knees bent up, feet flat on the floor. Or lie with your lower legs supported on a chair. Remember to relax!

Or you could try lying on your side, knees tucked up into the foetal position, possibly with a pillow between your knees (*see figure 2*).

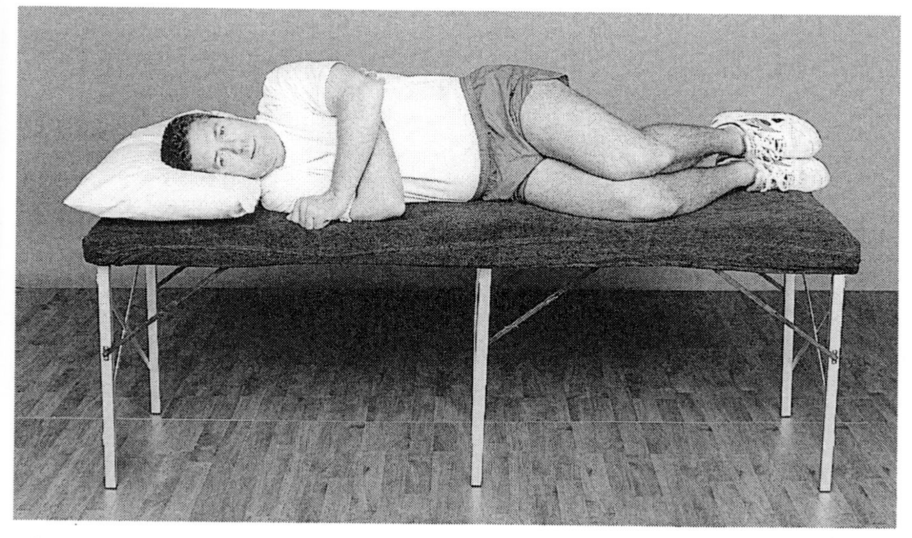

***Figure 2 Sidelying***

Relaxing is something that many people lose the ability to do well – particularly as they get older. Try the following:

1. **Lie on your back with a small pillow under your head and a pillow under your knees.**
2. **Take a deep breath in, and as you breathe out, 'let go' – do this three times in a row.**
3. **Now, focus in on your feet and think of them relaxing. If you feel they are not relaxed, then tense the muscles in them slightly and then 'let go'.**
4. **Now do the same with your other body parts, working from the feet up – lower legs, thighs, pelvis, abdomen, chest, lower back, hands, arms, neck and shoulders, face and scalp.**
5. **As you come to each area, if it is difficult to relax it, then just tense it up a little and then 'let it go'.**
6. **When you reach the head, you might want to start again, or let your mind go too – this is the hardest bit!**

If you practise this technique you will get better, until eventually you may find relaxation comes instantly on lying down. You can then practise doing it sitting up, which means you can do it anywhere! If this is an area you feel you need some work on in the long run, it would probably be best to go for lessons.

Getting up and turning over may be very sore as you're using the muscles that are causing you pain. However, you must move – it won't be sore for long!

1. **When getting up it's usually best to turn onto your side first.**
2. **Then use the upper hand to push against the surface you're on.**
3. **As you come up, swing your legs off the bed.**
4. **Get your breath back.**
5. **Grab onto something and stand straight up from the edge of the bed.**
6. ***Do not* lean forwards as you stand up.**

Once you know which position is most comfortable and how to relax then you should ... do some exercises!

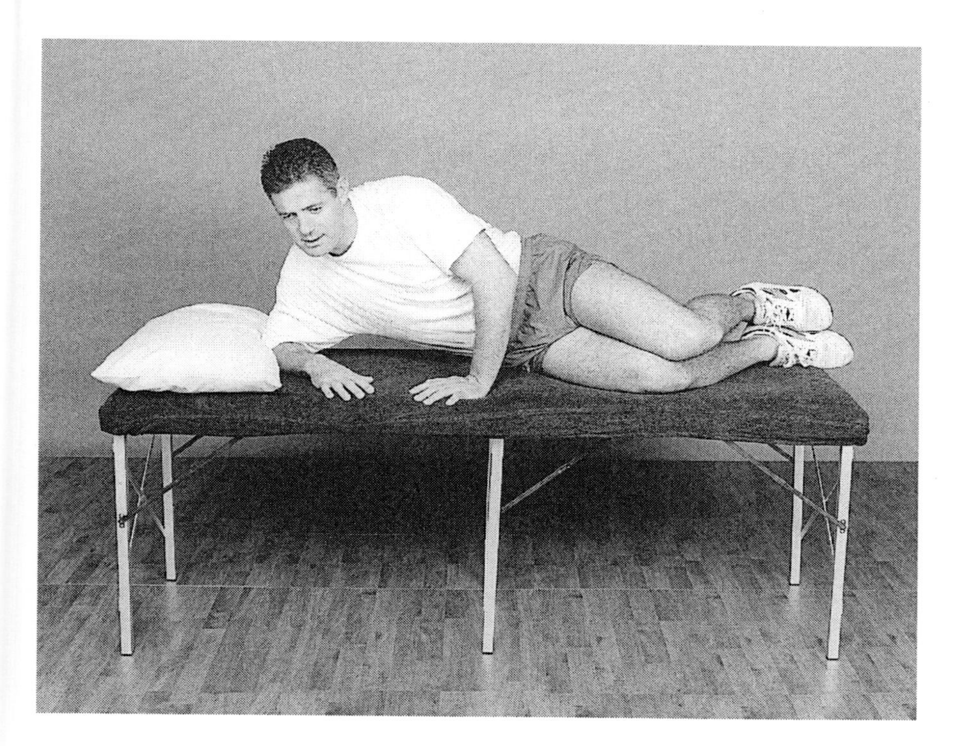

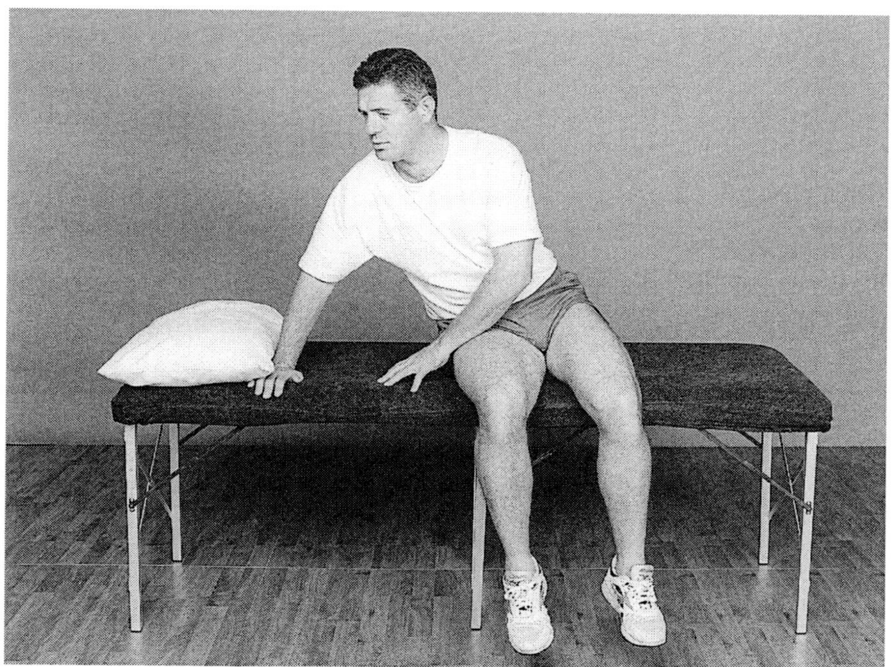

***Figure 3 Getting up from sidelying***

# Rest and Gentle Movement

- The Importance of Movement
- Which Movements To Do and How Many
- Rest and Exercise

## The Importance of Movement

**Use it or Lose it but don't ever Abuse it!**

It used to be thought that people with back pain should rest as much as possible. However, we now know that you should not rest (lie down) completely as this leads to a slower recovery and perhaps a less complete recovery. If your back pain is really agonizing it may be necessary to rest for 1 to 3 days, but generally no longer than this. If you are able to move around, even just a little, then move around.

- **If you don't move you'll soon stiffen up. So, have confidence and try to relax into the movements given here.**
- **If moving causes an agonizing pain then take a moment to relax, and try the movement again.**
- **No sudden movements – if you are getting repeated sharp jabs of pain it can set you back a bit. (Abuse!)**
- **If you can't move at all without agonizing pain, then call your GP out – he or she will be very understanding and will give you something for the pain (*see page 147*).**

You were given joints and muscles so that you could move the different parts of your body around, so do it **(Use it or Lose it).** Just be careful – follow the guidelines given below. The more you move, the more confidence you'll get and the more relaxed you'll be.

**A simple warning: if any of the exercises seem to make the pain worse don't do them so vigorously or don't do them at all. Do each movement *almost* to the point where it's uncomfortable and relax into it.**

## Which Exercises To Do and How Many

### SUPINE HIP FLEXION

1. Lie flat on your back on the floor.
2. Always move one leg up at a time, keeping the other flat down.
3. Bend one knee up and hold it, underneath the joint, with both hands.
4. Pull the knee up towards your chest.
5. Hold for 10 seconds
6. Lower the knee slowly back down until it is flat on the floor again.
7. Repeat with the other leg.

*Figure 4 Supine hip flexion*

## CRUCIFIX

1. Lie on your back with both knees bent up, feet flat on the floor.
2. Allow your knees to fall together to one side.
3. Relax like this for 30 seconds.
4. If this is sore, try resting your knees against something like a settee.
5. Don't allow your knees to go as far as the painful point, but find a point off centre that you can relax into.

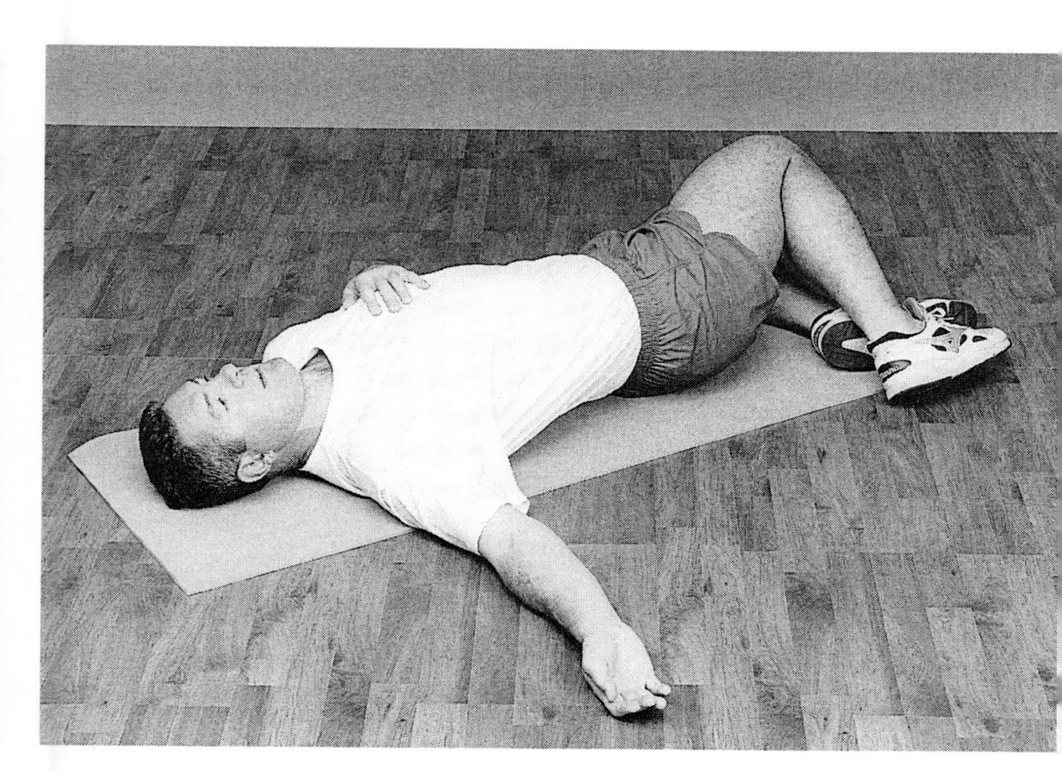

*Figure 5 Crucifix*

## LUMBAR TRACTION

1 Lie on your back on the floor with a pillow for your head.
2 Support your lower legs on a chair, with right angles at your knees and hips.
3 With your hands push both thighs down, towards the chair.
4 Breathe out while pushing and relax.

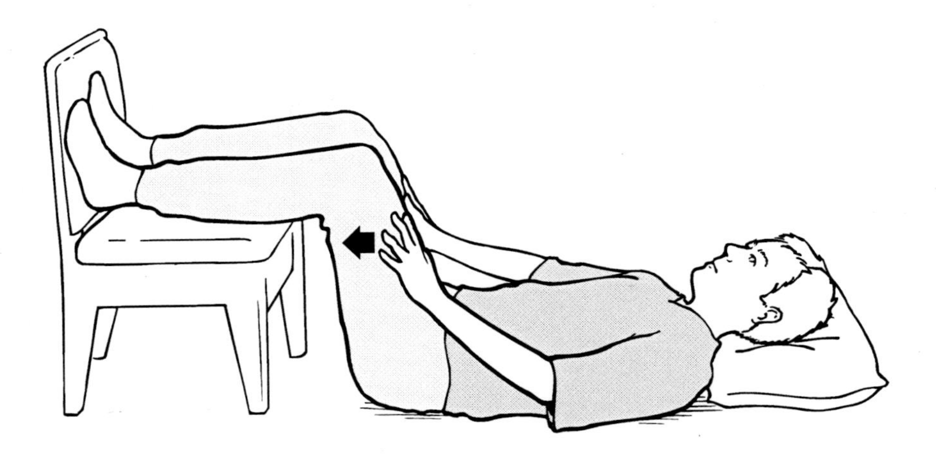

*Figure 6 Lumbar traction*

## LUMBAR FLEXION

1 Lie on your back, pull one knee up and hold it under the knee joint to avoid straining it.
2 Holding the first knee in position, pull the other knee up and grab hold of it as well.
3 Gently pull both knees up towards your chest until you feel a slight stretch in your lower back – no pain.
4 Rock gently in this position for 30 seconds.

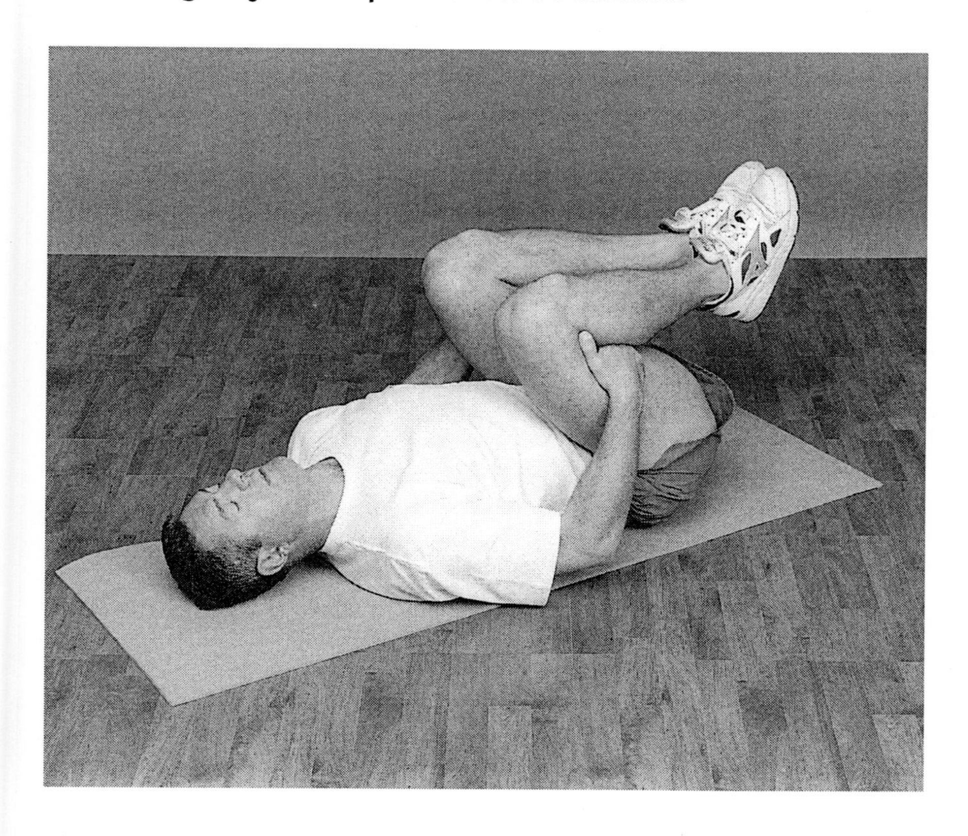

*Figure 7 Lumbar flexion*

## PELVIC TILTS

1. Lie on your back with both knees bent up, feet flat on the floor.
2. Tighten your stomach muscles so that your lower back flattens onto the floor and there is no gap between your lower back and the floor.
3. Relax and repeat at a rate of one every 5 seconds.

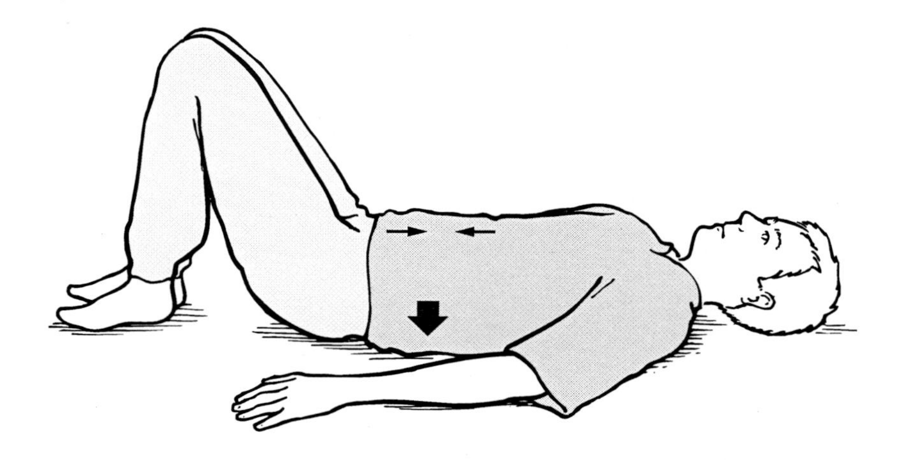

*Figure 8 Pelvic tilts*

Here is a suggested exercise routine to get you started:

| | |
|---|---|
| Hip flexion | Three each side, alternately, holding each for 10 seconds |
| Crucifix | Two each side, alternately, holding each for 30 seconds |
| Lumbar flexion | 20 in total, rocking gently |
| Pelvic tilts | 10 in total |

**If any one of these exercises is painful then don't do that one this time. But DO do the others! Try to build in more exercises as you feel able.**

To begin with, you should increase the frequency of your exercise sessions, but **not** the number of times you repeat each movement. As your pain eases, you can increase the number of pelvic tilts you do.

## Rest and Exercise

If you get the balance between rest and exercise right you'll get better a lot faster than if you don't.

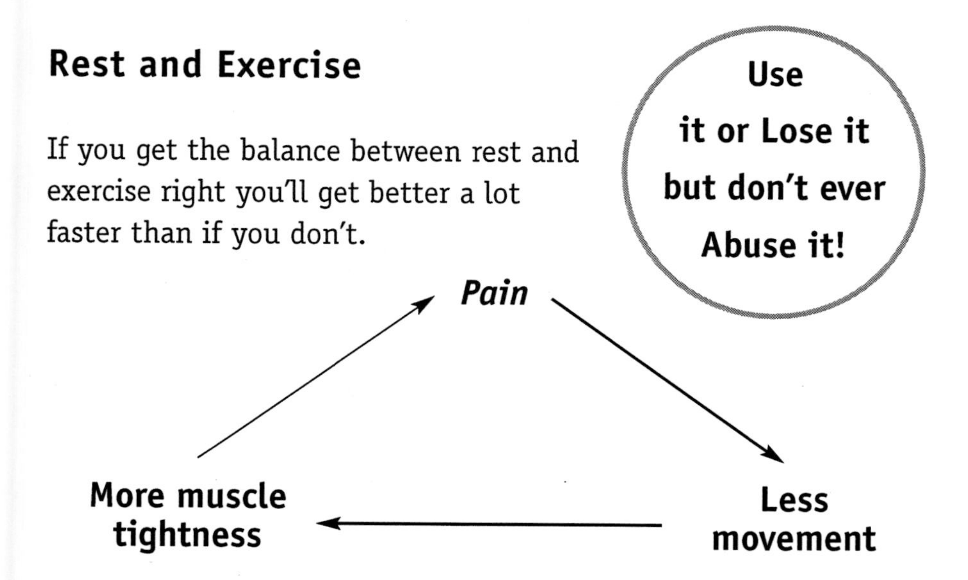

You need to change this to:

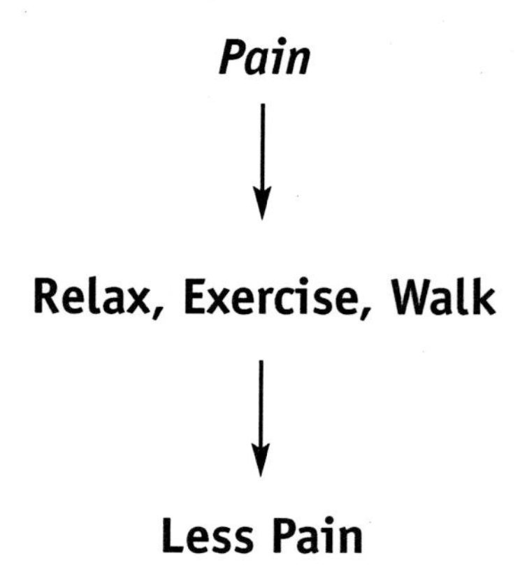


Try this programme:

1. **Relax lying down for 20 minutes.**
2. **Do some exercises.**
3. **Get up and walk around for 5 minutes.**
4. **Relax for 20 minutes.**
5. **Do some exercises.**
6. **Get up and walk around for 5 minutes.**

Remember: if it hurts more after you've done something, don't do it again, or do less of it so that it doesn't hurt again **(don't ever Abuse it)**. Do what you can – every little helps. As you improve, do a little bit more of the exercising and walking, but still take good relaxation breaks. See the 'Chronic Back Pain' section for more exercises – gradually build them into your programme.

# Hot and Cold

- When To Use Cold and When To Use Hot
- How To Prepare and Use an Ice Pack
- How To Prepare and Use a Heat Pack

## When To Use an Ice Pack

- If the pain is hot or throbbing.
- If you have just injured yourself, for the first 2–3 days.
- If heat seems to make the pain worse.

## How To Prepare an Ice Pack

- Use a plastic food bag with no holes.
- Fill the bottom with ice cubes – about ten should be enough.
- Add enough cold water to cover the ice cubes.
- Tie off the end of the bag.

(A bag of frozen peas – or other vegetables – is not as effective at staying cold.)

## How To Use an Ice Pack

- Cover the bag with a thin cloth (such as a tea towel) or oil your skin to protect yourself from ice burns.
- Place the ice pack over the throbbing pain – you may be able to secure it here by wrapping a towel around it and you.
- Leave on for 15–20 minutes and try to *relax*.
- Repeat every 1–2 hours.

Sometimes it's not obvious where to put the ice pack – for example, when pain is radiating right down the leg (*see Sciatica page 40*). Start with the ice pack at the small of your back and then move it towards the buttock if this seems to provide more relief.

## When To Use a Heat Pack

- **If you have an ache with occasional spasms or gripping pain.**
- **If cold seems to make the pain worse.**

## How To Prepare a Heat Pack

Use a hot water bottle at a comfortable heat.

## How To Use a Heat Pack

- **Apply in the same way as an ice pack – no oil necessary.**
- **You should usually find you're placing the heat to the side of the spine or over the buttock; the most common sites of muscle spasm.**
- **Leave on for 20–30 minutes and relax.**
- **Repeat every 2–3 hours.**

You may find that acute pains lasting more than 3 days respond better to 5 minutes heat followed immediately by 5 minutes cold, 5 minutes heat, 5 minutes cold, and so on.

Commercially produced ice/heat packs can be bought from many chemists. These can be heated in a microwave or pan of hot water, and cooled in the freezer. They are generally easier to use than preparing your own, and can be reused.

A hot bath may seem very inviting but getting back out of the bath could undo any benefit you gain from being in the bath. It may be better just to kneel in the bath to have a wash, as standing back up from sitting could prove to be very painful. You should make sure you have help at hand.

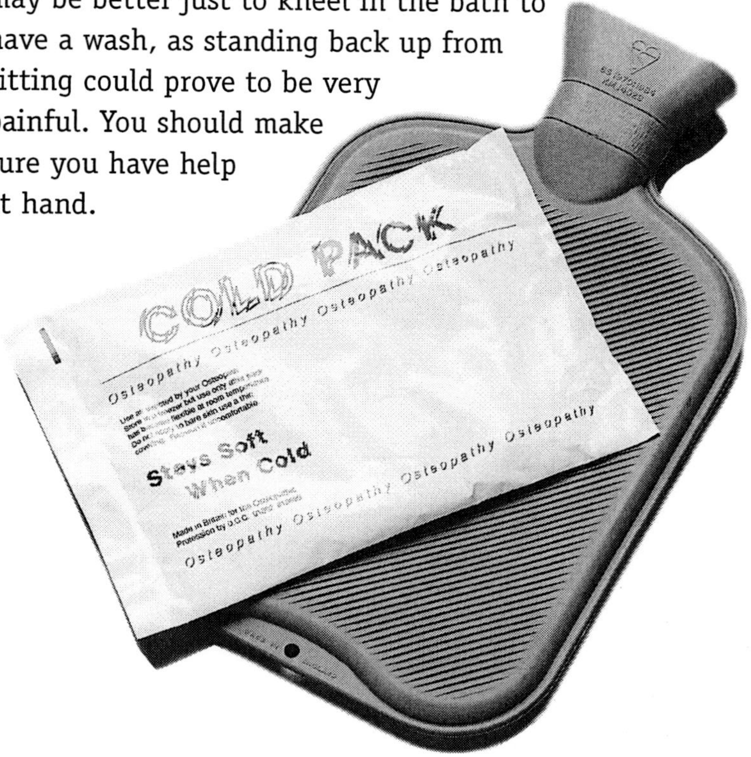

*Figure 9 A commercial ice pack and hot water bottle*

# Painkillers

(*See also page 147 on painkillers.*)

- **Should I Take Them?**
- **Should I Go To My Doctor?**
- **What Can My Doctor Do?**

## Should I Take Them?

- **If it's agony don't be a martyr – painkillers may help you to relax – YES! Try paracetamol as indicated on the packet, or aspirin.**
- **If the pain is bearable, painkillers may mask the fact that you're aggravating the problem – not a good idea – NO!**

## Should I Go To My Doctor?

Phone your doctor if:

- **Paracetamol or aspirin don't help and the pain is unbearable.**
- **You are having trouble with passing urine – urgency, difficulty starting, dribbling, increased frequency.**
- **You are experiencing any numbness (lack of feeling) under your bottom or a weakness in either of your legs.**
- **You are taking other drugs for other conditions (you can speak to your pharmacist about this).**

## What Can My Doctor Do?

Your doctor can:

- **Reassure you by examining you and making sure there is nothing 'terrible' wrong.**
- **Certify you unfit for work.**
- **Prescribe more powerful painkillers and/or anti-inflammatories or muscle relaxants.**
- **Refer you for NHS chiropractic, osteopathy or physiotherapy (though there may be a waiting period of several weeks) or to an orthopaedic consultant.**
- **Recommend a private chiropractor/osteopath/physiotherapist (who will usually see you within the week).**

# Lumbar Support Belts

- **What Is a Lumbar Support Belt?**
- **Will It Relieve My Back Pain?**
- **When Should I Use It?**
- **Where Do I Get One?**

## What Is a Lumbar Support Belt?

A lumbar support belt is a tight-fitting, broad, elasticated belt worn around your waist and upper hips (*see figure 10*).

## Will It Relieve My Back Pain?

- **By increasing your awareness of your movements it reminds you not to make sudden or strenuous movements and ensures that you move carefully, relieving your pain in the process.**
- **It helps to hold you up, relieving the load on your tired, spasmy back muscles and on your spinal column itself.**
- **It will not cure you, but will help you to get through the day.**

## When Should I Use It?

Use it all the time you are moving around to start with – other than when you are doing your exercises or when you are relaxing. As the pain eases, use the belt less. The people who sell you the belt should instruct you on how to wear it, but here are some guidelines:

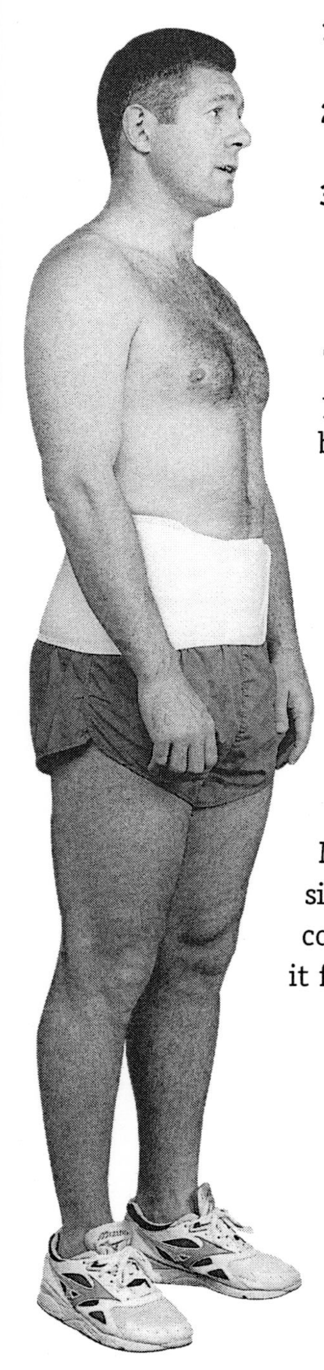

1. **Stand with the belt held behind you, holding one end in each fist.**
2. **Pull the ends straight out, away from your sides.**
3. **When at full stretch, pull the ends forwards around your waist, overlapping the Velcro bits at the front.**

This in itself can be hard to do well when you're in pain, but it's important that the belt is on tightly. It should cover the top half of your hip bones; if it's quite broad it will reach the bottom of your rib cage.

## Where Do I Get One?

You may be able to get one on loan from your GP. Otherwise, try phoning places like chemists and sports shops. Make sure you know your waist and hip sizes, and if you are not physically able to collect it yourself, make sure whoever gets it for you has this information.

***Figure 10 Wearing a support belt***

# Chiropractors, Osteopaths and Physiotherapists

- How Can They Help?
- What's the Difference?
- How Do I Find One and What Do I Look For?
- What is the Cost?

As soon as you are able to cope with getting in and out of the car, get off to see a chiropractor, osteopath or physiotherapist. The sooner the better. It's worth spending the money.

## How Can They Help?

These professionals are trained to diagnose and manage people suffering from back problems (and many other disorders). By diagnosing what is wrong with your back they will be able to reassure you, treat you using whatever means are most appropriate, give advice tailored to suit you, and help you with the exercises in this book. You do not need to get a referral from your GP to consult one of these professionals privately, although you may wish to discuss it with your GP: he or she may be able to recommend someone.

## What's the Difference?

(Definitions taken from the different professions' literature.)

**Chiropractic is a profession which specializes in the diagnosis, treatment and overall management of conditions which are due to mechanical dysfunction of joints.**

**Osteopathy focuses on the musculoskeletal system (bones, joints, ligaments, muscles and connective tissue) and the way in which this inter-relates with the body as a whole. It combines scientific knowledge of anatomy and physiology and clinical methods of investigation. Osteopaths diagnose and treat faults which occur because of injury or stress, allowing the body to restore itself to normal function. A caring approach and attention to the individual is considered particularly important.**

**Physiotherapy is a health care profession which emphasizes the use of physical approaches in the promotion, maintenance and restoration of an individual's physical, psychological and social well-being, encompassing variations in health status.**

You can see from the above definitions (if you can follow them!) that these are similar professions. Traditionally osteopathy and chiropractic are manipulative approaches to health care – the practitioners use their hands mostly. Physiotherapy has been more exercise-based and uses more electrotherapy (e.g. ultrasound). However, there has been a swing in recent years in physiotherapy toward more manipulative procedures. A recent study in Scotland into the similarities and differences between the three professions demonstrated that there were more differences within each profession than there were between them: the sort of treatment you get depends more on the individual practitioner. The important thing to establish when you decide to consult one of them is that they are used to working with people who have back problems.

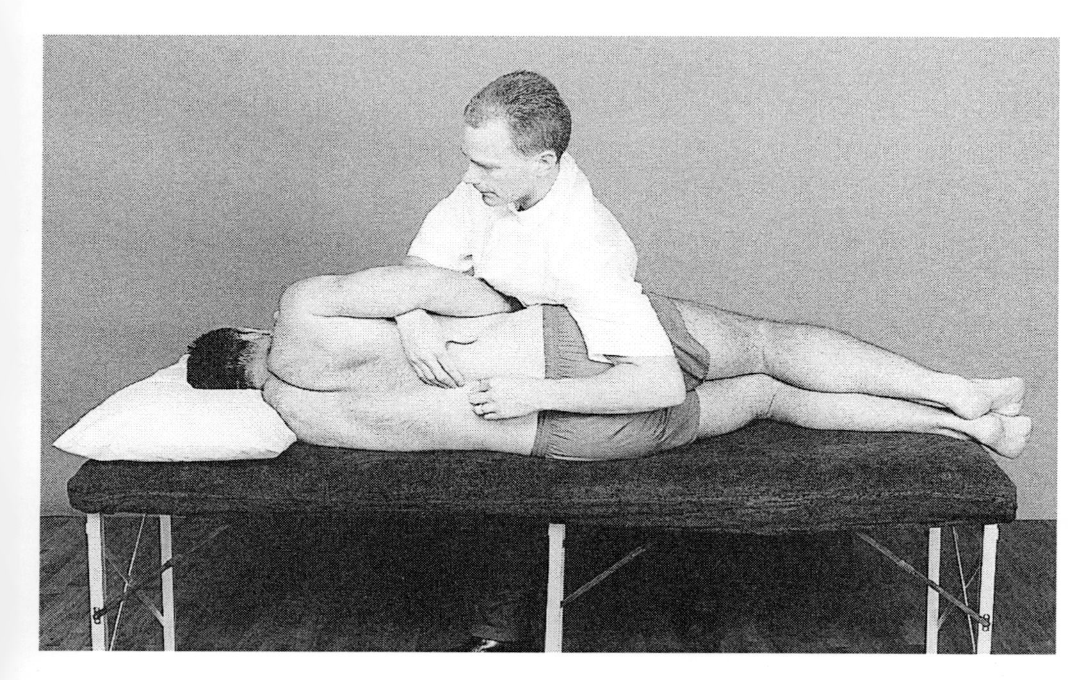

***Figure 11 An osteopath at work***

## How Do I Find One and What Do I Look For?

The ideal way to find one of these professionals is a recommendation from a friend. Most private practitioners will be listed in the Yellow Pages if you're desperate.

Osteopathy and chiropractic are over 100 years old and were first developed in America. Both professions were only practised in the private sector for the first 80 years in Britain. However, they are increasingly available through the NHS now, due to their popularity and the recognition given to them by other medical bodies. Osteopathy and chiropractic are going through a process of statutory registration. This means that anyone claiming to be an 'osteopath' or a 'chiropractor' should be on a newly-established register. This system ensures that all practitioners on these registers are well qualified and gives you the same guarantees of quality of care as if you went to see someone calling themselves 'doctor' or 'dentist'. Physiotherapy is not a profession governed by statutory registration, but the Chartered Society of Physiotherapy is a voluntary registration body whose members are well trained to deal with back problems – you should look for 'MCSP' after their names.

Main libraries will carry a register for each of these professions – ask the Librarian. The addresses and phone numbers of these bodies are given in the Appendix at the back of this book.

## What is the Cost?

Currently, the cost of a private consultation with a chiropractor, osteopath or physiotherapist is usually between £26 and £40. Sometimes one appointment is enough to make you feel 100%, but it is more common to need a few visits. This can easily add up to £100 or more. However, the true value should be seen in terms of how much better you feel. You wouldn't think twice about spending £100 on your car if it needed to be repaired. Sometimes your body needs a bit of help too! Your car's parts can be replaced with identical parts – your body's parts cannot. Even the best replacement hip joints are not nearly as good as the real thing, and at the moment there's no such thing as replacement spinal joints! So, bite the bullet and go and see someone who can help.

# The Essence of Getting Better

## Use It Or Lose It But Don't Ever Abuse It

This little rule is so important; and you should apply it ruthlessly to your main aim of getting better.

**Don't ever Abuse it.**

Anything that you do, or try to do, that obviously makes the pain worse is probably going to slow down your recovery rate. You **must** avoid these things because otherwise all the good things you are doing to help yourself will be cancelled out.

On the other hand ...

**Use it or Lose it.**

If you find there are certain things that you **can** do, which do not aggravate your pain, then carry on and do them. Without movement your joints slowly stiffen up, your muscles weaken, your circulation slows down and you become bored.

Common things to avoid (or at least do less of):

- **Sitting**
- **Standing**
- **Sporting activities**
- **Sexual intercourse**
- **Carrying**
- **Driving**

Make your own list.

## Should I Take Time Off Work?

People often ask, 'Should I go back to work?' The answer to this is, 'If you are as likely to aggravate your back at home as you are at work, then you may as well be at work.' If, on the other hand, you have to do things at work that will obviously aggravate your pain, and you can avoid doing those things at home, then you should stay off work until you are able to cope with those things again. However, put your time at home to good use – follow the advice in this book: do not just sit around.

The desire to get back to work is an admirable one, but if you push your back too hard you will only end up needing more time off than if you had given your back the 2 or 3 days it needed to begin with. Be sensible!

# Understanding Back Pain

# The Anatomy of Your Lower Back

- **Bones**
- **Muscles**
- **Nerves**
- **Blood vessels**

We will consider your lower back to be from your bottom ribs right down to the bottom of your pelvis.

## Bones

The spine is made up of 26 bones, with the smallest at the top and the largest at the bottom (roughly). The bones in the lower back are the five lumbar vertebrae, the sacrum and coccyx, and the two hip bones (*figures 12, 13*). These bones provide your body's framework and where they meet one another are the 'joints'.

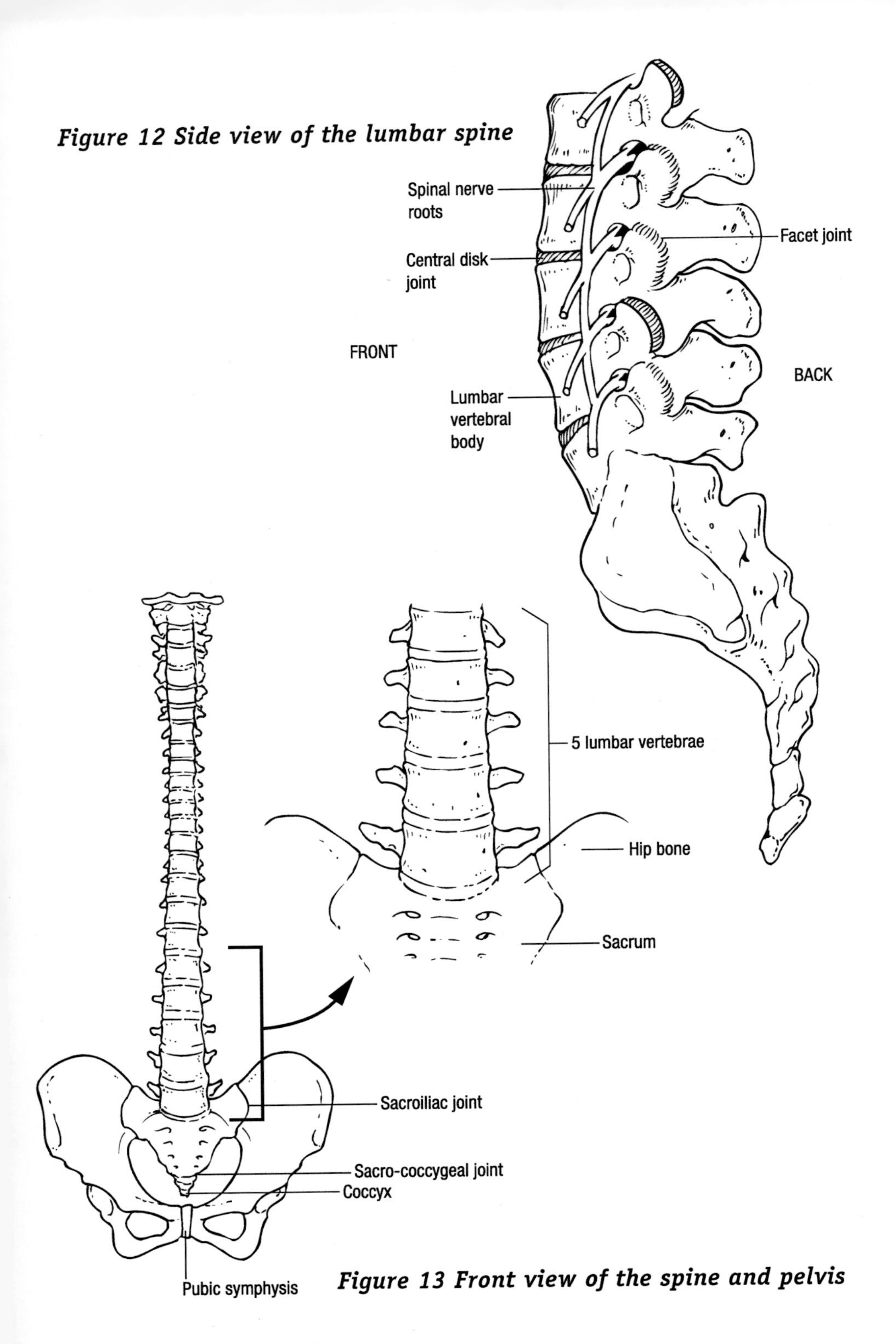


*Figure 12 Side view of the lumbar spine*

*Figure 13 Front view of the spine and pelvis*

## Joints and Discs

The joints are as follows:

- **Between the vertebrae – intervertebral joints.**
- **Between the spine and the hip bones – sacro-iliac joints.**
- **Between the two hip bones at the front – pubic symphysis.**
- **Between the sacrum and coccyx – sacro-coccygeal joint.**

### THE INTERVERTEBRAL JOINTS

There are two types of intervertebral joints:

**The Central Disc Joint (*see figure 14 and figure 12*)**
The discs are made up of tens of thousands of thin fibres, each connecting one bone to the next – this fibrous outer portion of the disc is called the annulus. In the centre is the nucleus, made of a firm, jelly-like substance. The whole disc looks a bit like the inside of an old golf ball with all those elastic bands wrapped around one another, except the fibres are much shorter and thinner.

**The Facet Joints (*see figure 12*)**
Facet joints are behind the disc joints and are much smaller joints. Here the bones are smooth and glide against one another. They are surrounded by ligaments. Ligaments are tough, slightly elastic bands of tissue designed to limit excessive movement at a joint.

### THE SACRO-ILIAC JOINTS (*SEE FIGURE 13*)

These joints are between the sacrum and the hip bones on each side. They move very little and are really there to transmit the weight of your trunk to the pelvis and through this down to the legs.

### THE PUBIC SYMPHYSIS (*SEE FIGURE 13*)

This joint is between the two hip bones where they meet at the front. There is a sort of 'disc' joining the two hip bones at this point, except that there is no 'nucleus' here.

### THE SACRO-COCCYGEAL JOINT (*SEE FIGURE 13*)

This is the joint between the sacrum and the coccyx. There is very little movement here. The joint is important though, particularly in childbirth when the tip of the coccyx must move backwards to allow the baby to pass out through the pelvic floor. Problems here often make sitting very uncomfortable, but this can be eased by sitting on a ring cushion – shaped like a toilet seat – to take the pressure off the coccyx.

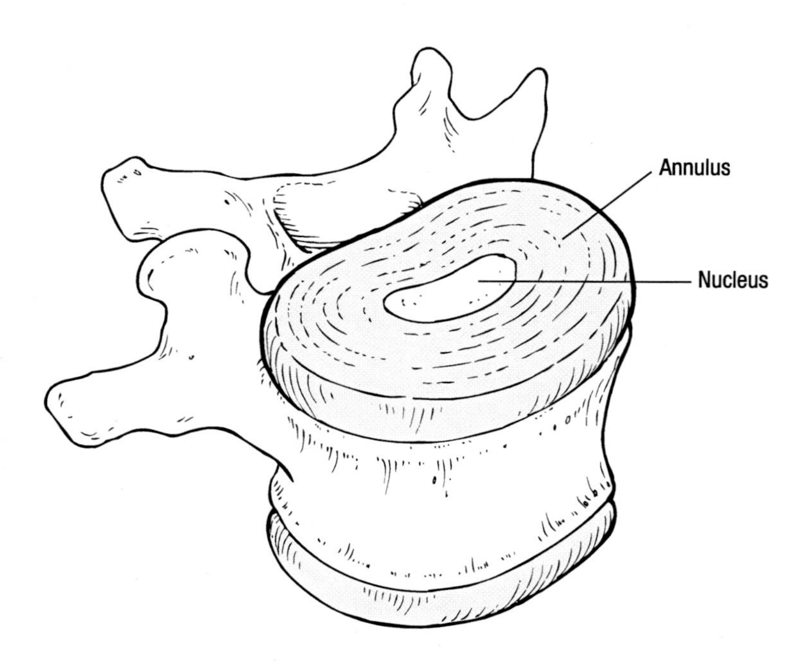


***Figure 14 A top view of a disc***

## Muscles

Muscles cover all these bones, each of the muscles attaching to two or more bones. The function of the muscle is to contract. When it does so, it pulls its two ends closer and the result is movement. It can also remain tense ensuring that the two ends do not separate (to hold your standing posture, for example); or it can lengthen slowly in a controlled way (as you bend forwards your back muscles elongate gradually, controlling this movement). Sometimes the end of a muscle, where it attaches to the bone, is called a tendon. Without your muscles you would not be able to move or hold any position – you'd just be a pile of bones and other softer bits on the ground.

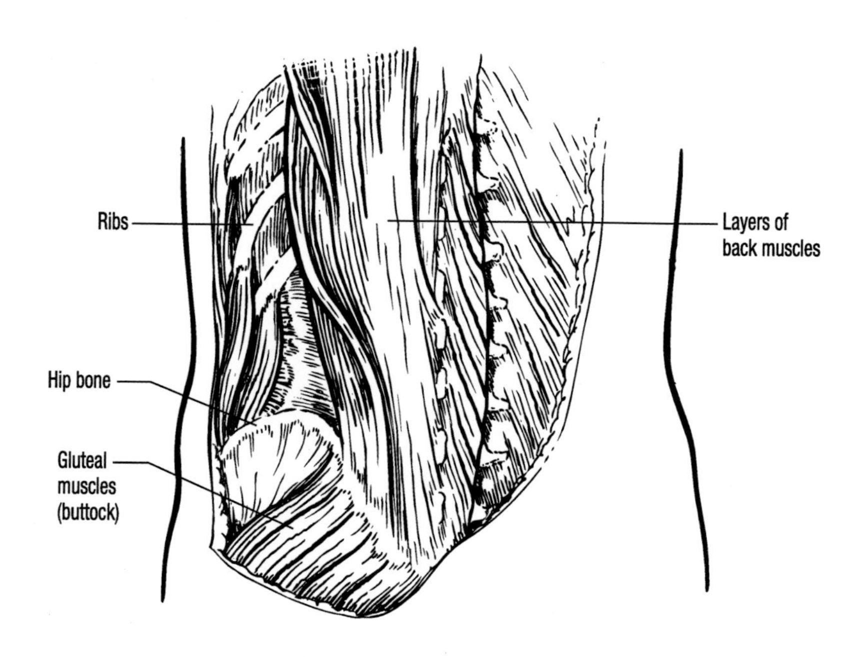


***Figure 15 The muscles of the low back and hips***

## Nerves

Nerves – like electric cables – transmit impulses along nerve fibres – like electric wires. Where a nerve fibre starts and where it ends determines what effect it has. The nerve fibres we're interested in are of two types.

- **Motor: end on a muscle, making it contract or just tighten, or relax.**
- **Sensory: end in your brain providing sensation.**

| *Motor Fibres* | *Sensory Fibres* |
|---|---|
| Come from spinal cord with connections to brain | Come from all tissues – skin, muscle, ligament, tendon |
| Messages pass from spinal cord to muscle | Many messages pass up to brain – pain, temperature, position, fine touch, pressure |
| Make muscle tighten or relax | Keep you updated with your body's changes |

A nerve is made up of thousands of nerve fibres, some motor and some sensory. So nerves like the sciatic nerve have a motor and a sensory function (*see figure* 16). It sends messages to the muscles to tighten or relax, and it keeps you updated of the changes going on in your leg.

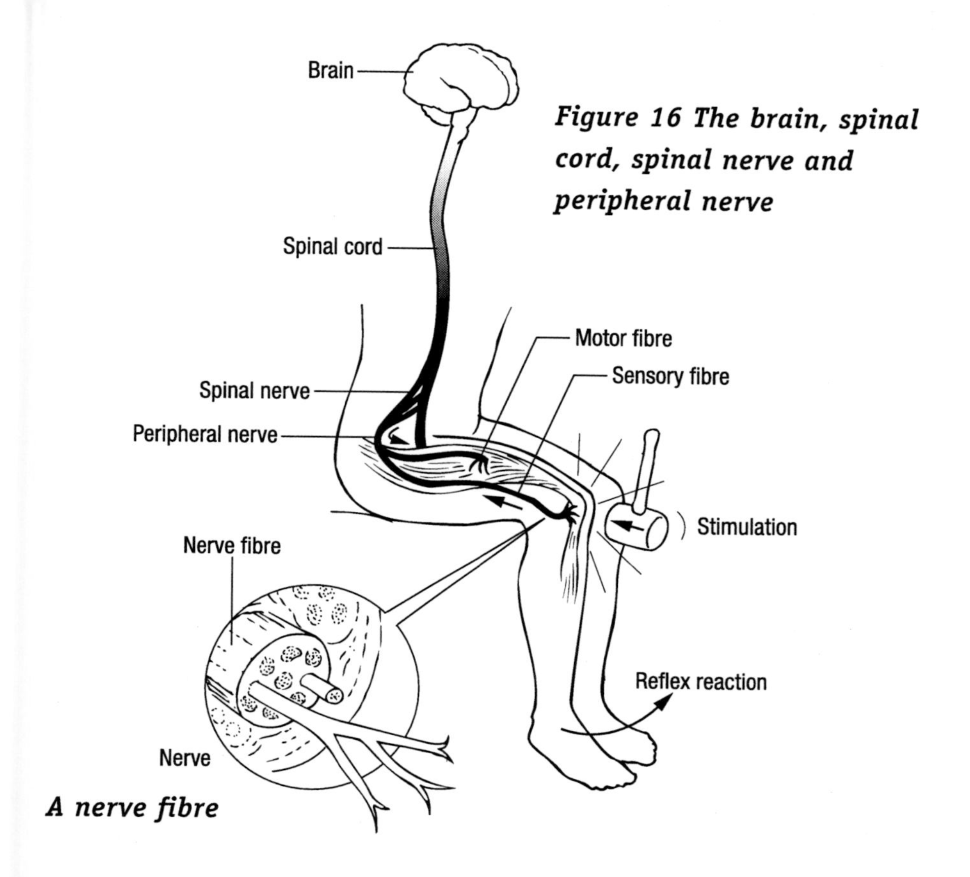


*Figure 16 The brain, spinal cord, spinal nerve and peripheral nerve*

*A nerve fibre*

## Blood Vessels

Blood vessels carry blood – **fresh blood** goes along the **arteries** to the various tissues (bone, disc, muscle, ligament etc.) from the heart and lungs; **used blood** goes back to the heart and lungs along **veins**. Blood carries lots of things that are essential for the smooth running of your body to the various tissues and removes waste products to be passed out of your body through your kidneys, bladder and lungs.

Without a good blood supply your tissues will not get a good supply of all the nutrients they need, including oxygen. Also, there will be a build up of lots of waste products such as carbon dioxide ($CO_2$) and lactic acid. This changes the balance of chemicals with the following results:

| | |
|---|---|
| Low level of oxygen. | Damaged tissues recover more slowly or not at all. Muscles tire more quickly and find it difficult to relax. |
| Low levels of building blocks for repair of damage. | Damaged tissues rebuild more slowly. |
| Increased acidity through high $CO_2$ and lactic acid. | Nerves become sensitized and are therefore more likely to send pain signals. Muscles prone to cramp and tiredness. |

But you may say, 'I don't suffer from high blood pressure or heart problems. There's nothing wrong with my blood vessels.' And you'd be right – and wrong! Remember that movement is essential to maintain good circulation – particularly drainage – of blood (Use it or Lose it). People frequently move less when they're in pain; the result is that the part of you which is moving less has poorer circulation of blood (and lymph – a tissue fluid).

Any of the tissues that have been mentioned may be damaged by acute injury leading to pain – this damage is usually tearing of fibres, whether they be muscle, ligament or disc fibres. Damage to tissues normally results in inflammation which is part of the healing process, but inflammation is painful. However, the sensation of pain is there to warn you that you have damaged something and that you should take things a bit easier (but not give in entirely).

During inflammation certain chemicals are released from your blood stream along with extra fluid – this causes some or all of the following:

- **Redness**
- **Swelling**
- **Heat**
- **Pain**

Sometimes, if the damage is bad enough, you may suffer muscle spasms. You will almost certainly suffer a tightening of the muscles around the damage. This tightening restricts the flow of blood and lymph and can lead to the vicious circle shown in figure 17. The best way to deal with this situation is:

**Use it or Lose it but don't ever Abuse it!**

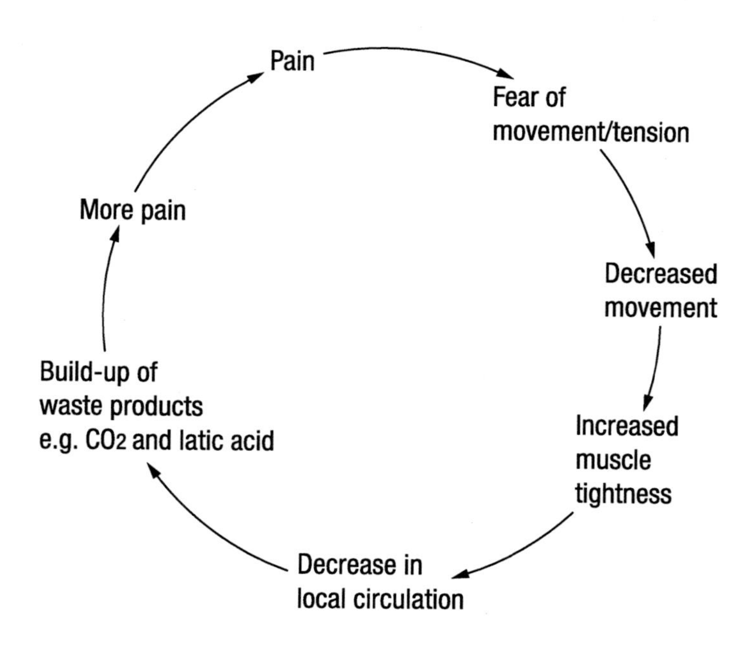


***Figure 17 The vicious circle of pain***

As far as blood flow goes, this rule is so important – if you just lie around or sit down, waiting for your pain to go away, your circulation will be much poorer than if you move around. As a result **you will take longer to get better!**

Sometimes (frequently) pain comes on gradually without any obvious injury. This is often a sure sign that you are mistreating your back in the way you use it (**abuse**). That is, you may have poor posture, not exercise enough or be lifting badly, i.e. you're abusing your back repeatedly! In this situation you are chronically straining your back and something (a muscle, ligament or joint) is protesting – pain! These types of problems, which have no obvious cause, can be difficult to deal with, but using a diary of your pain (*see page 69*) may help you to work out what the causes are. You may also wish to consult a chiropractor, osteopath or physiotherapist.

Both acute and chronic strains can lead to inflammation. In both situations the muscles and joints start to function in an unhealthy way and this can become your normal. If you allow this adaptation to continue you will end up with very different abilities to those you had before (**losing it**!).

As the muscles stay tight, so your movements are limited and your circulation is slowed down. This causes more stiffness and discomfort. You must make a conscious decision not to let this happen – **Use it or Lose it but don't ever Abuse it!**

**Good circulation is essential for good health and proper healing. Movement is essential for good circulation. So keep moving!**

# What Causes Pain?

- Pain Is a Sense
- Pain Is Complex – Why Your Leg May Hurt Too

## Pain Is a Sense

Pain is a sense, like sight and hearing, it tells you that something is wrong and that you should find out what. This message is transmitted along nerve fibres to a specific part of your brain (*see Nerves page 38*). There are very few parts of your body that do not send pain signals to your brain.

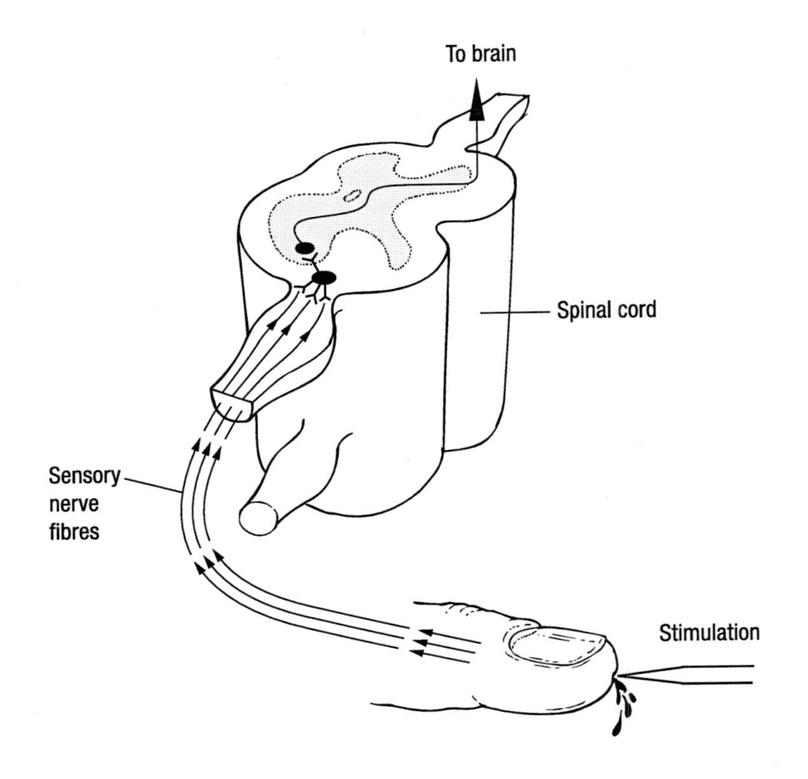


***Figure 19 A sensory nerve passing to the brain***

The sensation you feel as pain is generated by a part of your brain. This part of your brain is the end point for millions of nerve pathways from all over your body. The other end of the pathway is a simple sensory 'organ' (*see figure 19*).

This sensory organ is sensitive to pressure and/or chemical changes. So, a blow to one of these nerves will cause pain. Also, anything that causes the production of certain chemicals will cause pain – for example, inflammation, bruising or lack of (or poor) circulation. These cause a change in the chemical environment of a sensory organ that can sensitize it, so that normally painless movements become agonizing because you're stretching or pressurizing the sensitive nerves.

## Pain Is Complex – Why Your Leg May Hurt Too

'Referred pain' is what happens when you feel pain in one site, but it's coming from somewhere else – a bit like getting a crossed line on the telephone. This is very common, and can be confusing. Pain coming from the lower back can be felt in one or all of the following sites:

- **abdomen**
- **groin (including the testicles in men)**
- **buttock**
- **leg**
- **foot**
- **pelvic floor (up between legs)**

You may also feel tingling, or pins and needles. Sometimes people with lower back problems only experience pain in the leg.

Referred pain happens because your nervous system is complicated. The nerve that supplies sensation to your buttock may come from the same part of your spine as a nerve that goes to a facet joint in your back, so when you strain this joint you might feel all the pain in the buttock. There can be another reason for pain that comes from the back being felt in the leg, and that is a true 'trapped nerve' (*see page 54*).

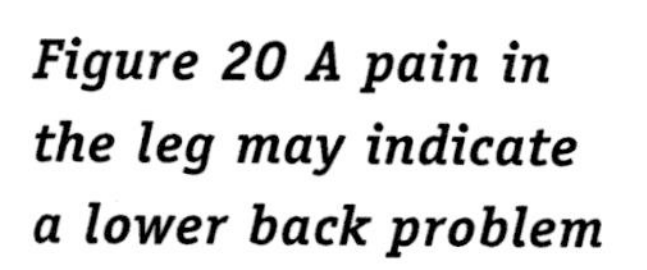

***Figure 20 A pain in the leg may indicate a lower back problem***

# The Real Diagnosis

- Muscle Spasms
- Scoliosis
- Strained Ligament
- Sciatica
- Lumbago
- Slipped Disc, Spondylosis, Osteoarthrosis and the Ageing Back
- Arthritis
- Trapped Nerve
- Coccyx Pain (Coccydynia)
- Osteoporosis

## Muscle Spasms

A muscle spasm is a gripping, agonizing pain that stops you in your tracks. It usually occurs following a movement, for example, bending over. Muscle spasms occur in various different back problems: you can injure any one of many different structures in your back that can lead to you suffering painful muscle spasms. This is your body's primitive but effective way of stopping you from doing any more! It is an involuntary action (one that you have little control over). Unfortunately it slows down the flow of blood and other tissue fluids which in turn leads to more pain due to a build up of certain chemicals, and can delay healing. It is vital to relieve this muscle spasm in order for function to return to normal. Also, if the original injury is aggravated by increased pressure (like a trapped nerve) then the chances are that muscle spasm may cause more pain as it increases the pressure on the damaged tissue and this sets up a vicious cycle of pain, muscle spasm, pain and so on. (*See Relaxation page 3*).

## Scoliosis

A scoliosis is a twist in the spine. When viewed from the back the spine will be bent to one side. Often there is an 'S' bend in the spine. One shoulder is frequently lower than the other. There are several possible causes for a scoliosis:

- **Congenital: You are born with it, probably due to poorly formed bones in the spine.**
- **Developmental: This comes on as you grow, again usually due to uneven growth of vertebral bone, or perhaps because one leg is longer than the other.**
- **Functional: This means there is something you do frequently that causes over-development of one side of your body creating a twist in the spine.**
- **Protective: If you have an acute injury (e.g. strained ligament, disc herniation) the muscle spasm pulls you over to one side in order to protect the damaged tissue.**

## Strained Ligament

A ligament is a tough, slightly elastic tissue that binds the bones together at a joint. It can be strained by over-stretching it. A ligament on the left side of the spine is most likely to be strained by forced bending to the right and forwards. This type of injury always results in muscle spasm, which in turn results in a protective scoliosis. This happens in an attempt to remove the pressure from the ligament – making sure it is not stretched again.

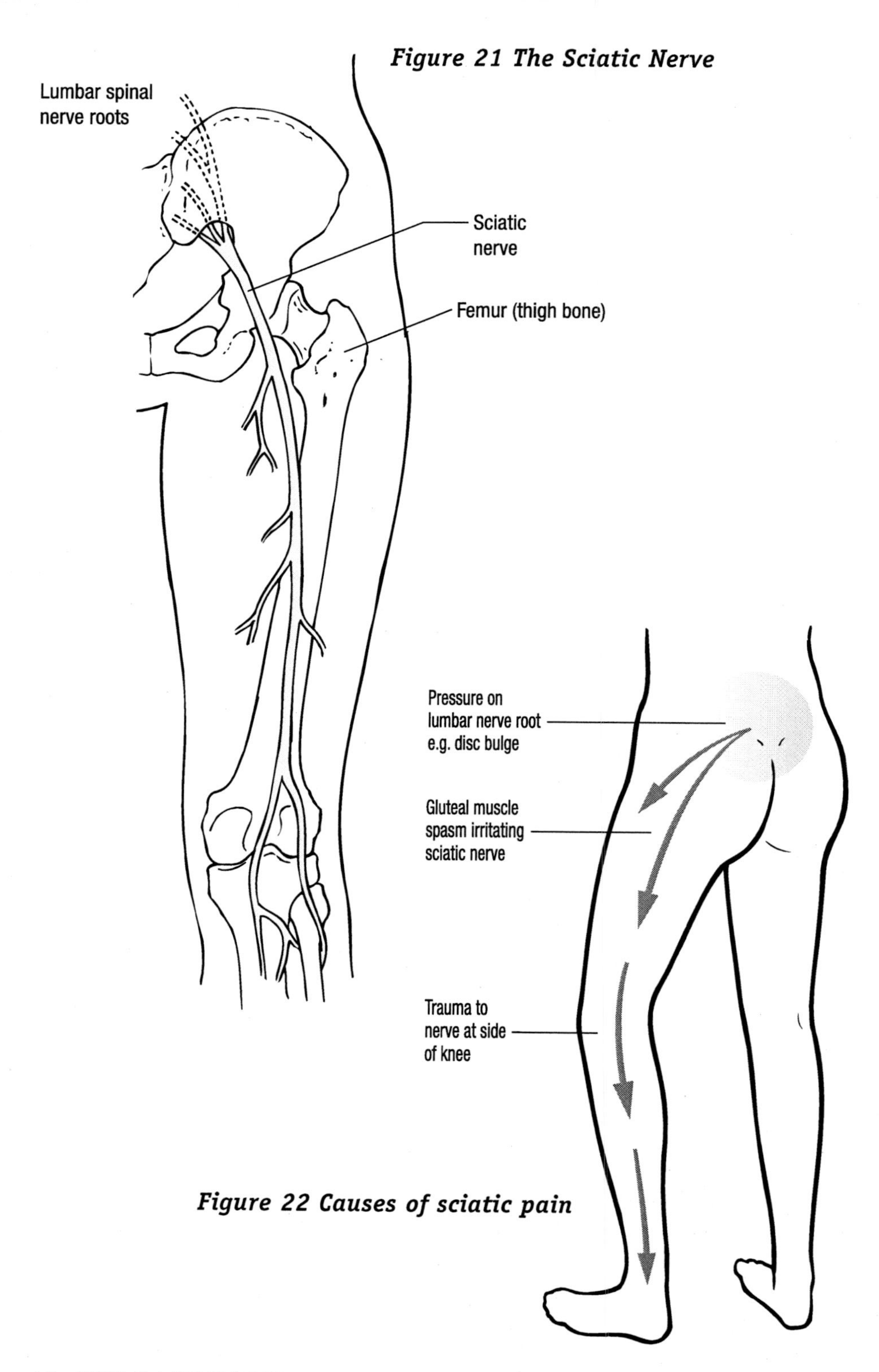


*Figure 21 The Sciatic Nerve*

*Figure 22 Causes of sciatic pain*

## 'Sciatica'

Sciatica means pain (or pins and needles or numbness) along the sciatic nerve. This nerve is made up originally by four spinal nerves (like tributaries of a river), and irritating any one of these spinal nerves or the sciatic nerve itself can cause sciatica. Figure 21 shows the course of the sciatic nerve. Figure 22 shows the most common sites for sciatica to originate from.

## Lumbago

Lumbago could alternatively be explained as, 'You've got a sore back and I don't exactly know why, except that it's not terribly serious.' 'Lumbago' simply means pain in the lumbar region of your back. This 'diagnosis' tells you nothing you don't already know!

## Slipped Disc, Spondylosis, Osteoarthrosis and the Ageing Back

- **Anatomy of the Bones, Discs and Nerves of the Lower Spine**
- **Slipped Disc**
- **Spondylosis, Osteoarthrosis and the Ageing Back**

### ANATOMY OF THE LOWER SPINE

On the following page is a picture of the lumbar spine showing the relationships between the bones, discs and nerves in the lumbar spine. The discs are made of millions of thin fibres wrapped around a soft centre – a bit like the inside of a golf ball (*see figure 24*). Don't forget that all this is surrounded and supported by muscles.

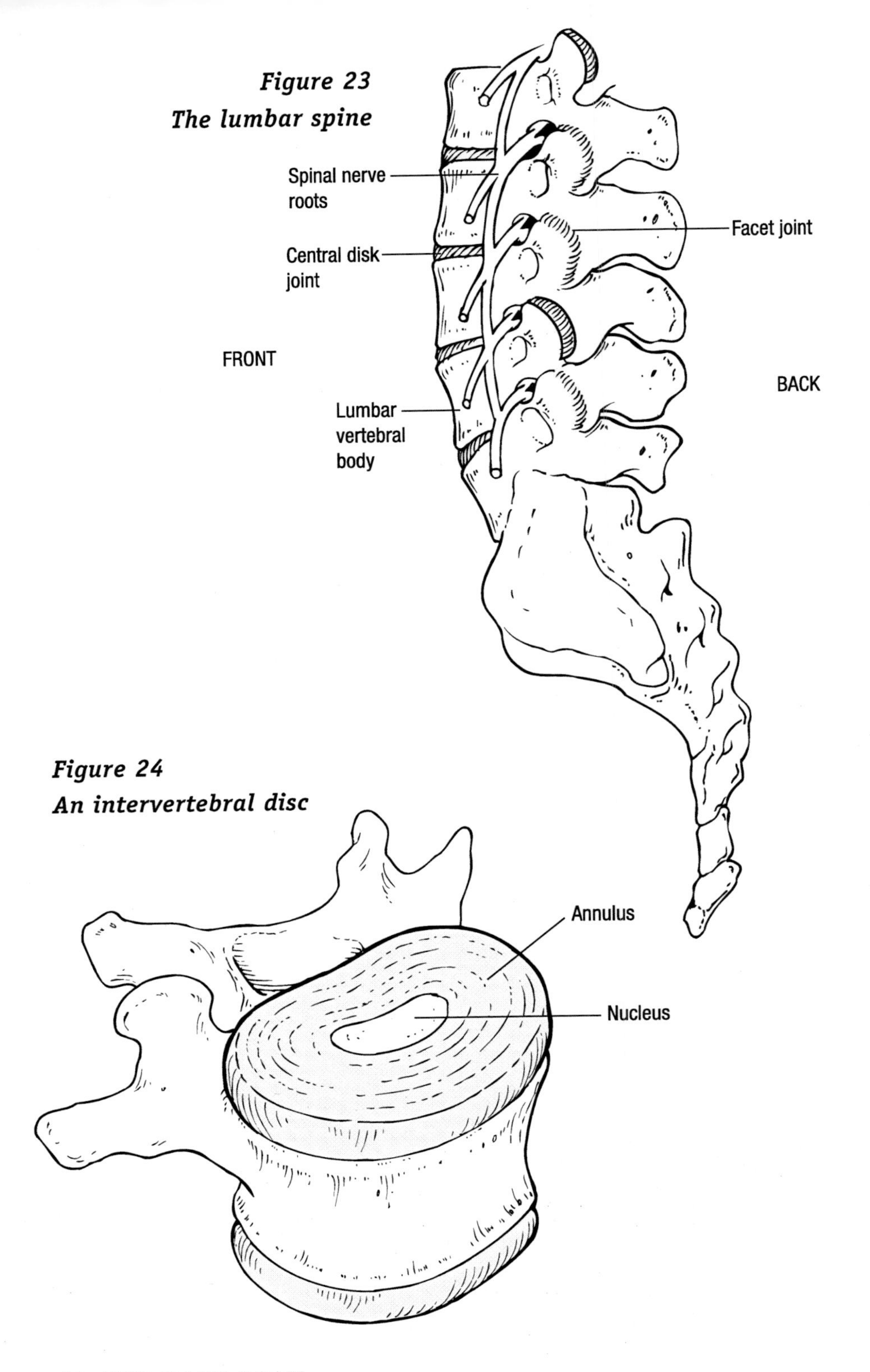


*Figure 23*
*The lumbar spine*

*Figure 24*
*An intervertebral disc*

## SLIPPED DISC

This term should be banned because discs do not 'slip'. They bulge or rupture – some of the annular fibres tear and the pressure inside pushes the remains of the disc out; a bit like the inner tube of a tyre pushing out through a tear in the outer tyre, distorting the shape. Disc bulges can push on one of the spinal nerves, irritating it and leading to 'sciatica'. Frequently, when a disc is injured the initial injury is painless or mildly painful. It is only once the injury becomes inflamed and muscle spasm sets in (a few hours later) that it becomes much more painful. The disc usually bulges backwards in one of its corners – this puts pressure on the nerve which passes out between the vertebrae at this point. The pressure on the nerve and inflammation cause pain and/or pins and needles to be felt anywhere along the length of this spinal nerve (sciatica) – *see figure 21*.

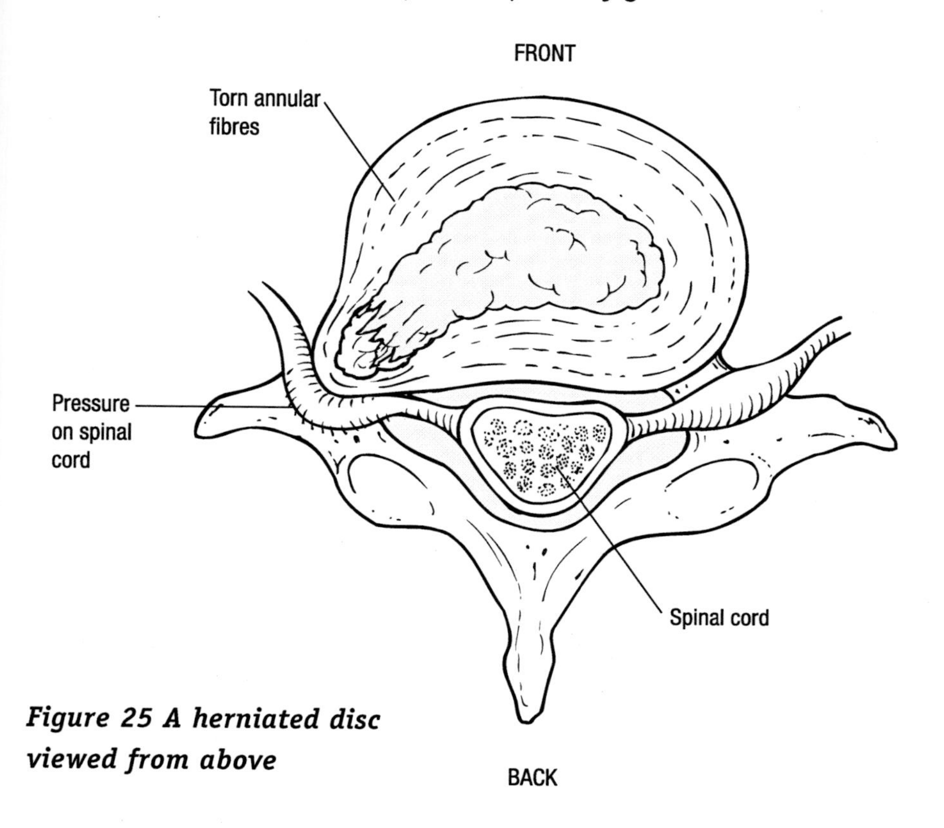


***Figure 25 A herniated disc viewed from above***

*Figure 26 A prolapsed disc*

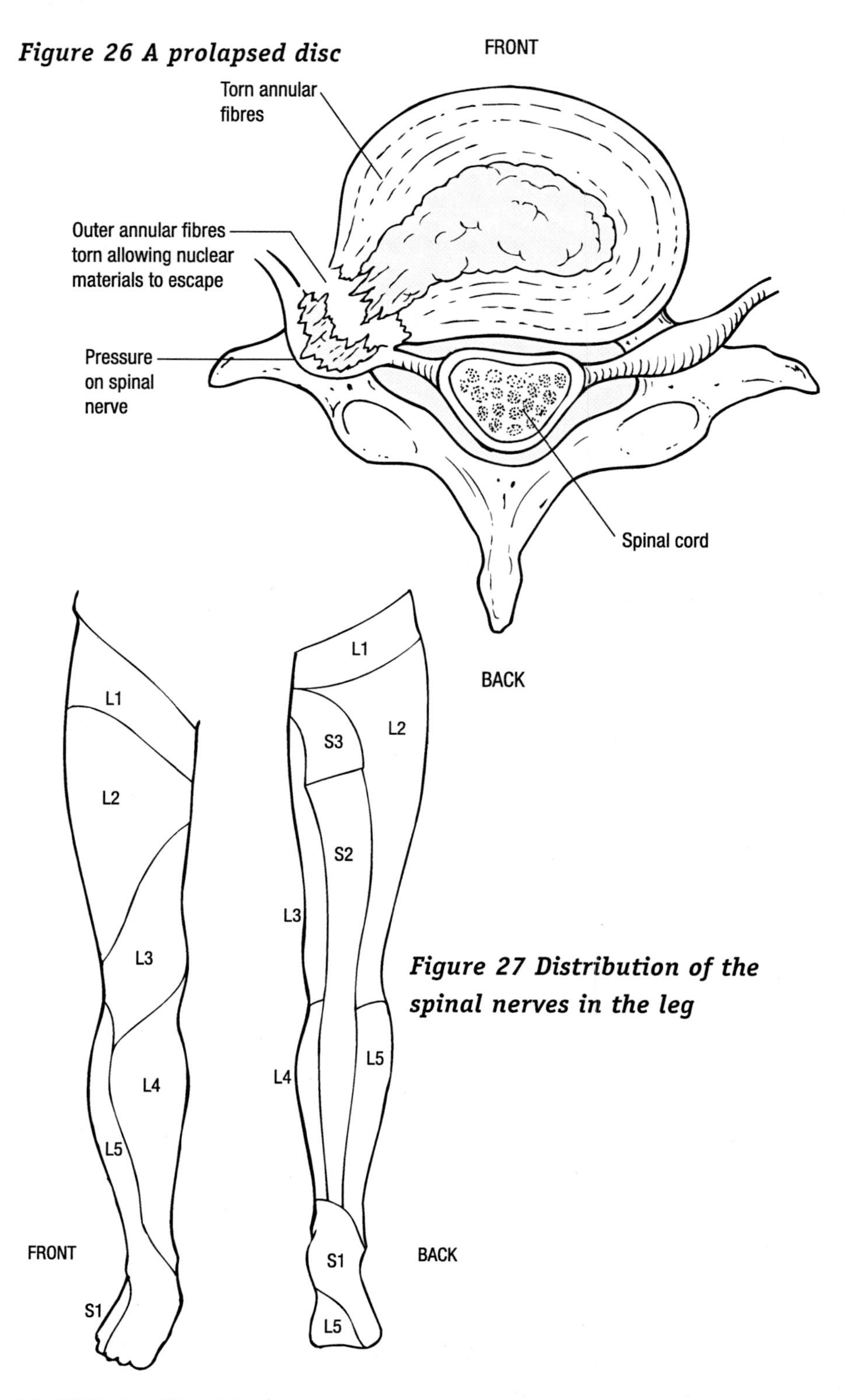


*Figure 27 Distribution of the spinal nerves in the leg*

## SPONDYLOSIS, OSTEOARTHROSIS AND THE AGEING BACK

As discs age they flatten and become slightly irregular. The bones come closer together and the disc is less able to cope with the forces it used to cope with when thicker and younger. It is more prone to injury and becoming inflamed. The bones themselves become irregular, with odd bits growing off around the edges. This is a natural degenerative process and may also be called osteoarthrosis. It may be speeded up by traumas such as rugby injuries or driving on bumpy surfaces. If this leads to tissue irritation and inflammation it may be called spondylitis or osteoarthritis (the 'itis' means inflammation). The smaller facet joints at the back of the spinal column also undergo this degenerative change resulting in slightly distorted joints. This ageing of the bones and joints also affects the softer tissues – the muscles tend to become smaller and tire more quickly, and the ligaments tend to become thinner and not so strong making them more easily strained.

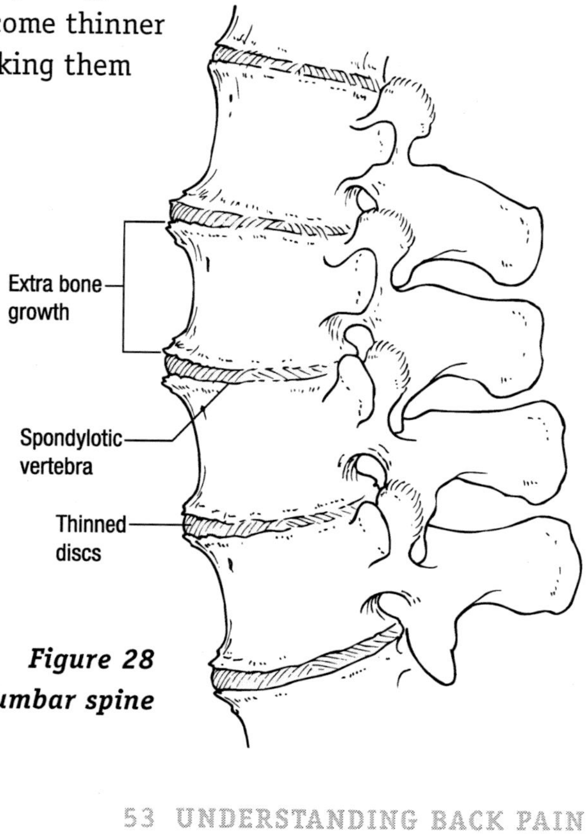

Extra bone growth

Spondylotic vertebra

Thinned discs

***Figure 28***
***Spondylotic lumbar spine***

## Arthritis

There are different types of arthritis; the one described above is osteoarthritis, which is the type that most commonly affects the back. The other types are part of a disease process that can cause inflammation in many different joints of the body. This process of inflammation is what causes the pain and destruction of the joints. Here is a list of the types of arthritis which most commonly affect the spine. These can only be diagnosed confidently with the help of blood tests.

- **Rheumatoid arthritis**
- **Psoriatic arthritis**
- **Ankylosing spondylitis**

While a lot of the advice given in this book may help people with these disorders, you should seek the advice of a doctor, chiropractor, osteopath or physiotherapist. *See the Recommended Reading on page 155.*

## 'Trapped Nerve'

Nerves – both spinal and peripheral (like the sciatic nerve) – can become 'trapped' by few structures and at few sites. The most common site is where a spinal nerve exits the spine and it is most commonly trapped or pressurized by a disc herniation or prolapse.

## Coccyx Pain (Coccydynia)

The coccyx and its joint with the sacrum are most commonly damaged by a fall straight onto the bottom, where you land in the sitting position. The pain tends to be limited to very low down just above and behind your anus. However, pain can also be referred to this point from the joint between the sacrum and the fifth lumbar vertebra. Frequently coccydynia is worse sitting upright because there is direct pressure on the coccyx. This can be relieved by sitting on a ring cushion.

## Osteoporosis

This is generally a disease of old age, more common in women than men. Essentially this is where the bony substance becomes less dense and so more prone to breaking. We all tend to lose bony matter as we age, but some people lose more than others. Often this does not cause a problem, and because of this it is frequently painless. The first thing many women know of it is when they fall and break a wrist all too easily, or they have an x-ray for something and the radiologist reports that the bones are a bit osteoporotic. This process doesn't only affect the spine – hip and wrist fractures are very common.

In its advanced stages, the whole spine tends to get shorter and the person loses height. The following factors are recognized as increasing the likelihood that you will suffer osteoporosis:

- **Family history of osteoporosis**
- **Late puberty**
- **Early menopause**
- **Other chronic medical conditions e.g. rheumatoid arthritis**
- **Smoking**
- **High doses of steroids**
- **Extended periods of bed rest**
- **Prolonged spells without periods (common in those suffering from anorexia nervosa).**

You should discuss the management of this problem with your doctor and chiropractor, osteopath or physiotherapist. You may find the book *The Osteoporosis Handbook* very useful in explaining this problem in more detail (*see Recommended Reading, page 155*).

The recovery time from the various problems detailed above varies greatly from person to person. It is not unknown for people to take years to recover from a disc injury – and yet a very fit and otherwise healthy rugby player may play a match with a herniated or prolapsed disc without any obvious problems. The main difference between the two is likely to be level of fitness and the consequent ability of the body to 'cope' with the weakness. This highlights the importance of an overall management plan to help you to regain as much movement and strength as possible – this is dealt with in the final section of this book.

Often the original injury is so long in the past that it is no longer very important. You have accommodated this injury by changing what you do, and in adapting you have caused more 'bad patterns' of movement which are now the source of your pain.

So, don't get too bogged down in the diagnosis. Although it's always nice to have a diagnosis, sometimes it can hold you back mentally. Remember, it's not what's wrong with your back that's important so much as what effect it has on your life.

Some people have terrible wear and tear on x-ray (spondylosis) and no pain at all; others may have very little wear and tear on x-ray and be told that their pain is due to this and they'll just have to live with it: 'there's nothing that can be done'. Which person do you think has a better quality of life? So don't concentrate too much on the diagnosis; pay more attention to how you feel and what you *are* able to do.

**Don't worry about the diagnosis – just how you feel!**

# Exploding the Myths

## Myth Number One

*The worse the pain, the longer it takes to get better.*

Some people can be in agony (due to muscle spasm) in the morning and be virtually pain-free by bedtime.

## Myth Number Two

*Once a bad back, always a bad back.*

Not with this book!

## Myth Number Three

*Slipped discs can be popped back in.*

Not the case, because they do not 'slip'. *See Slipped Discs, page 49.*

## Myth Number Four

*No pain no gain*

Rubbish – often pain is a sign that you're making things worse!

It is not the aim of this book to provide you with the correct diagnosis – just be assured that the majority of readers will improve if the advice in this book is followed. If you are not improving, go and see a chiropractor, osteopath or physiotherapist for a full assessment and diagnosis.

# Chronic Back Pain

# Motivation

If you really want to rid yourself of back pain – read this.

Is your back pain restricting your activities?

Do you want to suffer less back pain?

Are you willing to work for this goal?

If the answer to the last question is 'no' – sell this book to a friend!

If the answer is 'YES' then read on!

FACT – It is your back pain.

FACT – Just reading this book will not make your back better.

FACT – You must act on what you learn here.

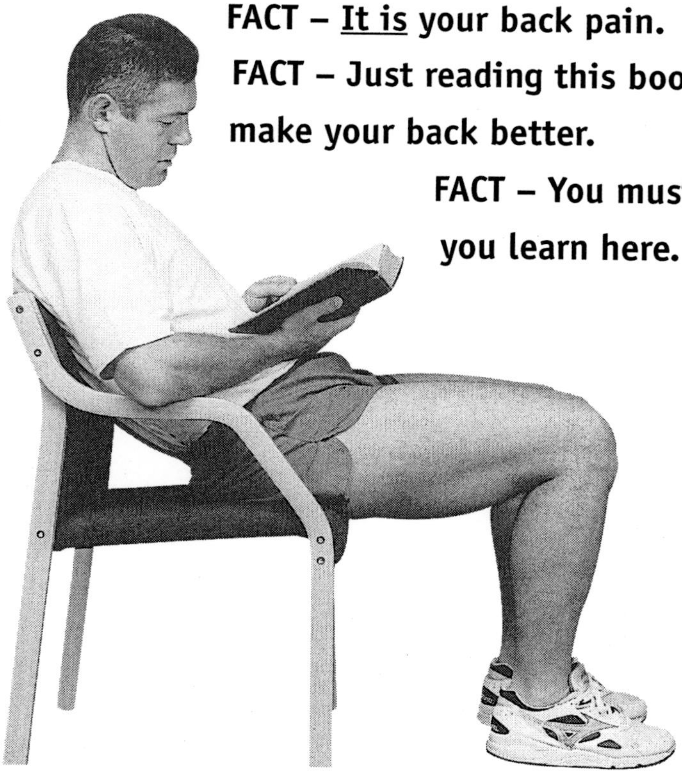

Human beings are frequently lazy – we often try to get by on the minimum work. If you take this attitude over a chronic back problem, you will probably always have a back problem.

If I stood over you all the time and kicked you in the back every time you were lazy with your posture or failed to do your exercises, you'd soon learn and make these things routine. Because your back pain comes and goes you forget the importance of following the advice given to you. In this section of the book we are trying to get you to change your habits – avoiding the bad habits and practising the good habits.

To help you do this we'd like to give you a tool to help you motivate yourself. So, take four sheets of blank A4 paper, and in big bold letters write the following:

**SHEET 1** **How you feel when your back pain is at its worst e.g. agony, frustrated, afraid, angry, useless. Now write down as many times (dates) that you can remember feeling like this as you can, particularly including the most recent time.**

**SHEET 2** **Everyday things you can't do when your back is at its worst e.g. walk, put on socks, do your job, climb stairs, get out of a chair, stand, bend, lift, turn in bed.**

**SHEET 3** **The things you would love to be able to do again, and would do if your back wasn't sore. A specific activity or event you would like to enjoy – be realistic for this one. If you've suffered back pain for more than a year, perhaps give yourself a date one year from reading this book by which time you would like to have achieved this goal.**

**SHEET 4** **Write down your intention to find out which bits of advice in this book are most necessary for you to get better, and to act on them. Write down what this advice is on sheet four and write down your commitment to this.**

If you or someone close to you notices your good habits slipping, look at what you've written and use those fears and desires to prick you back into action. Doing this may seem a little childish, but a written desire and intention is far more powerful than an unwritten one, particularly if you refer back to it frequently.

This is a technique used by successful sports and business people all over the world. For most people this written exercise is vital to secure their commitment to the goal – it's your contract with yourself. It puts your commitment down in black and white. Without this written contract many people let their good habits slide and without really being aware of it they end up back where they started. You must give yourself the best chance of carrying this 'programme' through to your written goal.

If you merely think to yourself 'Oh yes, won't that be great? A better back. Yes, I really fancy that, I'll give that a go,' it's all too easy to let things slide. You must be committed to this – how much does it matter to you? Do you really want to suffer less back pain? When setting your sights on a worthwhile goal, write it down – you don't have to share it with anyone; keep it private. If you merely dream of being pain free, it will always remain exactly that – a dream. If you think of it as achievable, and something you desperately want, give yourself the best chance:

- **Write your goal down.**
- **Write down your commitment to the goal.**
- **Give yourself a time frame over which to achieve this goal.**

Now, write in your diary a time when you will look at these four sheets of paper every two days for the next month, then every two weeks for the following six months, and then every month thereafter. If you combine this strategy with the advice and exercises given in this book you are giving yourself the best possible chance of being a lot better a year from now – and isn't that why you're reading this book?

Do you want to continue to be one of the tens of thousands of people in this country who are classed as 'chronic back pain sufferers'? Do you want to be one of the people who cause their GP's eyes to glaze over the minute you open your mouth? If not:

**_You_ must do something about it!**

If you need help with your back problem – in the shape of a chiropractor, osteopath or physiotherapist (*see page 24*) – don't think of this purely as an expense; think of it as an investment. If you have a weak back it could cost you your whole standard of living if you don't sort it out. A 'bad back' could mean the end of your career. Or it could at least mean having to change your job – how many nurses do you think have to give up nursing due to a bad back? So, don't always think of the cost of treatment or exercising – think of the value of it in the long term.

Even if you were one of the very few people who benefits from surgery (*see page 142*) for back problems, you would still need to do exercises, practise good habits and avoid bad habits to give yourself the best chance of getting rid of your back pain.

- **If you are feeling down at any time, look back and see how far you've come.**
- **Do not worry if you cannot manage to exercise every day, just make sure you're doing your best!**
- **When you start a programme of exercise, or you try to alter your posture, you may find that your back becomes more uncomfortable for the first week or two – do not let this put you off. Your muscles and joints have to get used to moving in unaccustomed ways, and as they do things will get easier. If they do not, or the pain is severe, consult a chiropractor, osteopath or physiotherapist.**

# Good Versus Bad Habits

- The Problem – The Cliff of Pain
- The Plan

**15%**
**of adults are chronic low back pain sufferers – do you want to be one of them?**

## The Problem

Too many people regard their back pain as due to one isolated incident – one thing they did (lifting the shopping out of the boot or bending over the bath). In reality, this is usually just the last straw. There are normally lots of different things which have contributed to you reaching this point – and all these different factors need to be addressed. Do you accept that if you were fitter – more supple and stronger – then your back would be less likely to 'go' under the same circumstances? As for those of you who suffered a gradual onset of back pain, this is a pretty good indicator that something you do on a regular basis has led you to this point. So, back pain is usually due to many different things building up over a period of time – pushing you closer to going over the edge, resulting in low back pain – *see figure 30*.

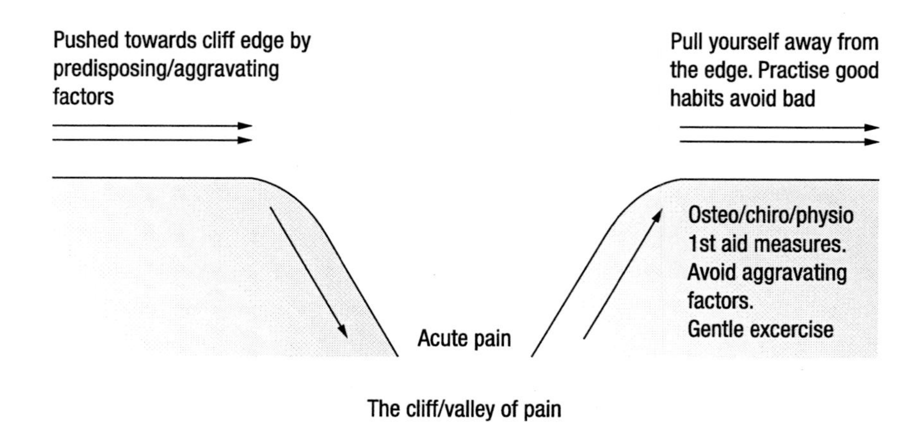


*Figure 30 The cliff of pain*

## The Plan

The plan of action for improving your back is shown opposite. As you can see, it is a simple process to summarize. However, YOU have to follow it! Good health – and this includes improving your back problems – is always a balance of doing enough of the positive and as little as possible of the negative; we don't expect you to be perfect, just swing the balance in favour of positive, rather than negative factors.

**START POINT**

↓

**Bad Back**

↓

**Avoid bad habits (aggravating/maintaining factors)**

*decrease negative factors*

↓

**Chiropractor, osteopath or physiotherapist**

*positive*

↓

**Good posture**

*positive*

↓

**Good exercise programme**

*positive*

↓

**Improve general health**

*positive*

↓

**Address diet, stress, smoking**

*decrease negative factors*

↓

**Good Back (Good Health)**

↓

**END POINT**

# Avoiding the Bad

- Aggravating/Maintaining Factors
- Keeping a Diary
- Avoidance

## Aggravating/Maintaining Factors

An aggravating factor is something that makes your back more sore than before – this can be difficult to assess if you are taking pain-relieving medication. On a sheet of A4 paper list all the things that seem to increase the pain. Listed here are some common ones.

- **Sitting**
- **Standing**
- **Running**
- **Walking**
- **Sexual intercourse**
- **Driving**

## Keeping a Diary

Keep a diary of how you feel and all your activities for a week or two. Look back through the diary to see what may be aggravating your back pain, and do something about it! Update your aggravating/maintaining list! Shown in figure 31 is an example from a diary.

| | | |
|---|---|---|
| 7am | got up | stiff sore low back, R leg pain eased after 30 mins |
| housework, ironing | | |
| 1pm | Lunch | Not bad during morning, very sore R leg after sitting for 1 hour @ lunch |
| shopping | | |
| 6pm | Dinner | leg been sore all afternoon, eased after lay for half hour and took 2 aspirin |
| 11pm | Bed | Not bad – lay on floor, watching TV |

***Figure 31 A diary of pain***

## Avoidance

If something very strongly aggravates your back pain you MUST avoid it. Otherwise it's a bit like saying 'I've got a really bad headache, but I can't discuss it now as I'm too busy banging my head against this wall.' If something mildly aggravates your back pain you MUST do less of it, for the same reason. Ask yourself again – do you **want** to get better?

What about **'No pain no gain'**? – Rubbish! For most back problems you need to minimize the painful things. Some of your exercises may be strenuous and hard to do at first but they should not cause you to feel more pain.

It may be that if you consult a chiropractor, osteopath or physiotherapist you are given advice which conflicts with that given here. We have not diagnosed what is wrong with your back so your therapist is better placed to give you advice. However, anything which very obviously makes your back pain worse is stopping you from getting better – this seems like common sense. As we have said in other places in this book, you can slowly reintroduce these activities.

# Bad Posture and Good Posture

- **Standing**
- **Shoes**
- **Sitting**
- **Lying**

Good posture is different for different people – we all have different skeletons and so we will all have slightly different postures.

So, you can have good posture standing, sitting or lying. When you are moving around you also need to be aware of your posture. Your skeleton (the bones and the joints in between them) is built in such a way that the bones fit one another, and are all supported one on top of the other when standing and sitting. However, without your muscles the whole lot would just collapse. Your muscles act as the guy ropes would on a tent frame – holding the whole lot upright by pulling evenly on all sides.

**Good posture is the position in which the different parts of your body are held in such a way as to minimize the strain on all the parts.**

One of the important functions of muscles is to relieve the strain on your joints (particularly ligaments) by holding you in the 'right' position. If you have a lazy posture, although this may feel easier for you to maintain (because there is little muscular effort), it is in fact damaging your joints. Too much muscular effort (the military posture) is just as likely to do damage!

Changing your posture – particularly standing and sitting postures – is nearly always hard. You've probably never dramatically altered your posture since you were a teenager, so all the muscles which hold you up have been used to working in this particular way. To change this takes a lot of conscious effort (to change your habits) and hard work (working muscles that aren't used to working).

However, remember – Use it or Lose it but don't ever Abuse it! If you sit, stand or lie in a 'bad' way, this is abuse and will do you harm. If you don't stand upright, and you slump all the time you will gradually lose the ability to stand upright. People who slump their shoulders forward (for whatever reason) tend to develop a curve in their upper backs and put their necks under increased pressure – these people gradually lose the ability to look up or bend backwards because they've spent so much time looking at the ground.

Posture is often affected by how you're feeling. How is your posture affected if you're depressed and tired? If you feel your mental well-being is a factor in your posture, perhaps you should consult someone about this.

## Standing

When you are standing well:

- **Your weight should be evenly distributed between your two feet.**
- **There should be even pressure between the heel and ball of your foot.**
- **Both knees should be fairly straight with the knee caps 'loose'.**
- **Abdominal muscles should be working but not rigid.**
- **Shoulders should be back and relaxed (not pulled back).**
- **Head high with chin down.**
- **Now – relax in this position! Don't sag!**

You should be able to balance a book on your head in this position. Unless you have a lumpy head!

A good tip is to think of someone pulling a hair on the top of the back of your head straight up. This lengthens your spine, pulling everything in and up.

So remember, your muscles need to work to keep you upright – if they're too lazy you will lean to one side or backwards or forwards. If the muscles on one side of you are overactive compared to the other side they will pull you off to one side (this sometimes happens in order to protect damaged tissue and can be a good thing). This uneven pull on parts of your body results in stresses and strains beyond the normal call of duty and this in turn leads to these tissues tiring and starting to cause pain.

*Figure 32*

***Bad standing posture***

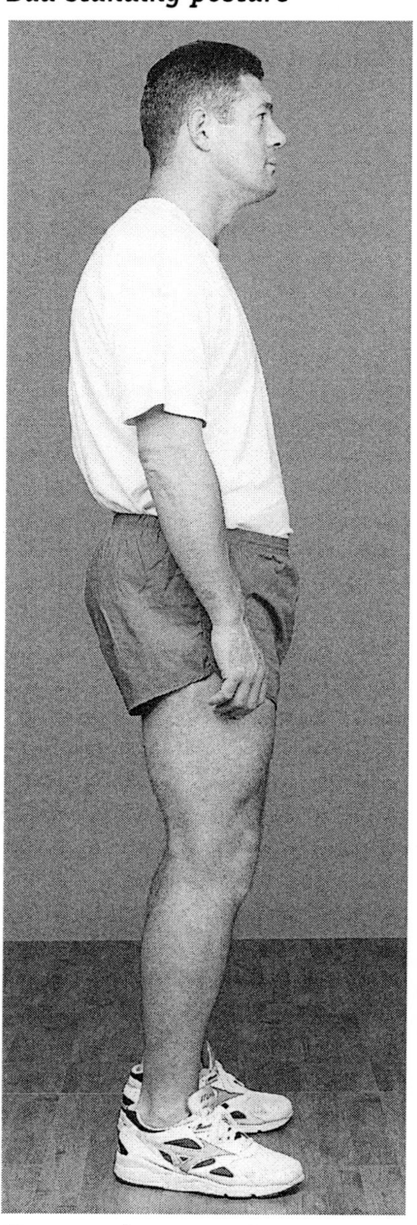

*No muscular support*
*No abdominal muscle effort*
*Shoulders rounded forwards*
*Head forward of body*
*Knees locked*

***Good standing posture***

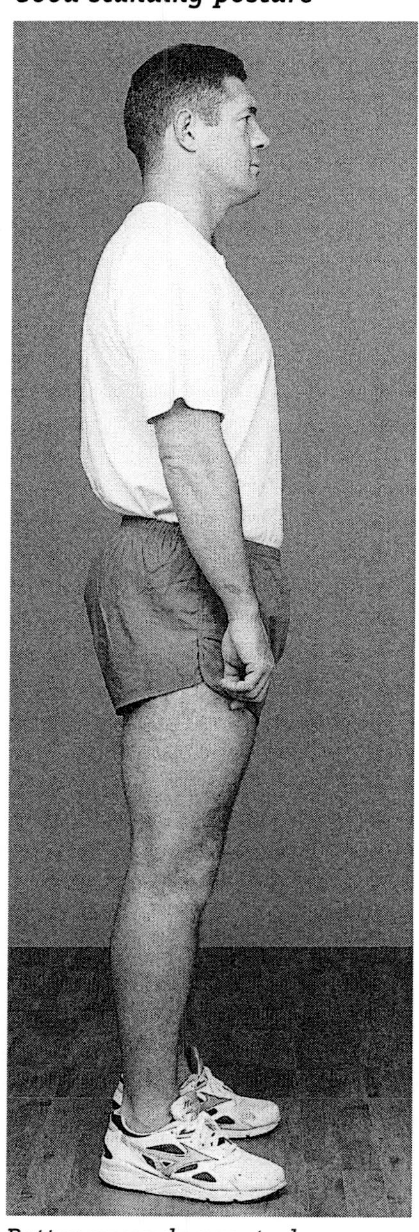

*Better muscular control*
*Abdominal muscles supporting*
*Shoulders relaxed*
*Head up and chin down*
*Knees straight, not locked*

*Figure 33*

***Bad posture (Military bearing)***

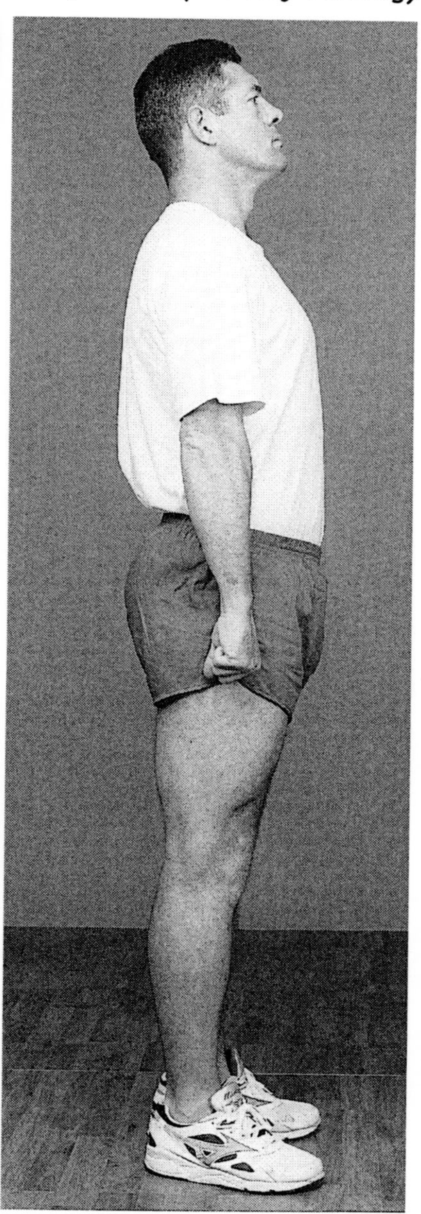

*Tense muscles*
*Military bearing of shoulders*

*Buttocks clenched*
*Thighs and knee caps locked*

***Good posture***

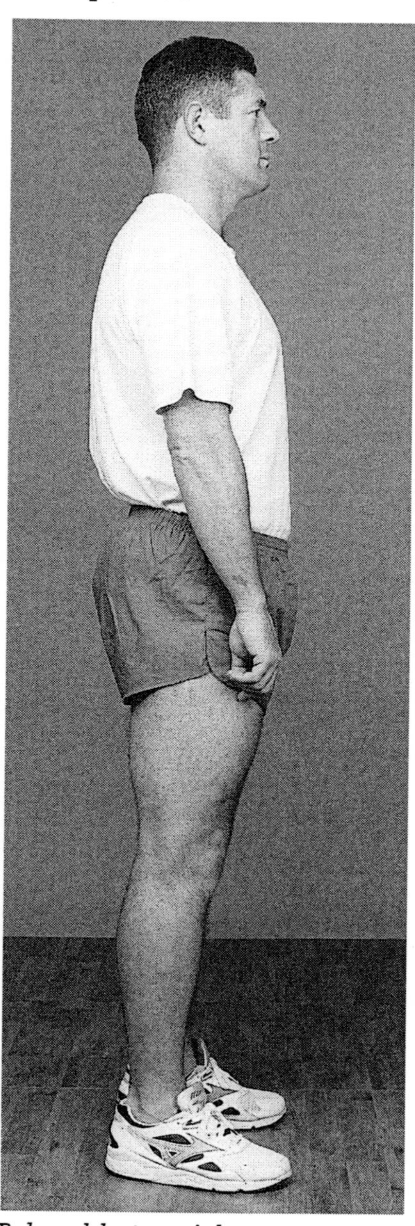

*Relaxed but upright*
*Shoulders relaxed but not rounded*
*Buttocks relaxed*
*Thighs and knee caps relaxed*

Some people habitually stand on one hip (*see figure* 34) which creates an uneven force not just on the lower back but on the whole muscular and skeletal framework – some bits will feel fine with this posture and some bits will start to protest. Because your lower back is the first bit above your hip bones, it is often your lower back that suffers first from the strain of standing unevenly. It may even be that you have one leg a bit longer than the other! This is a bit of a disadvantage but is not that unusual. If you think you may have different leg lengths go and see a chiropractor, osteopath or physiotherapist – they'll tell you one way or another, and although they cannot make uneven legs the same length, they will be able to help your body cope with this situation.

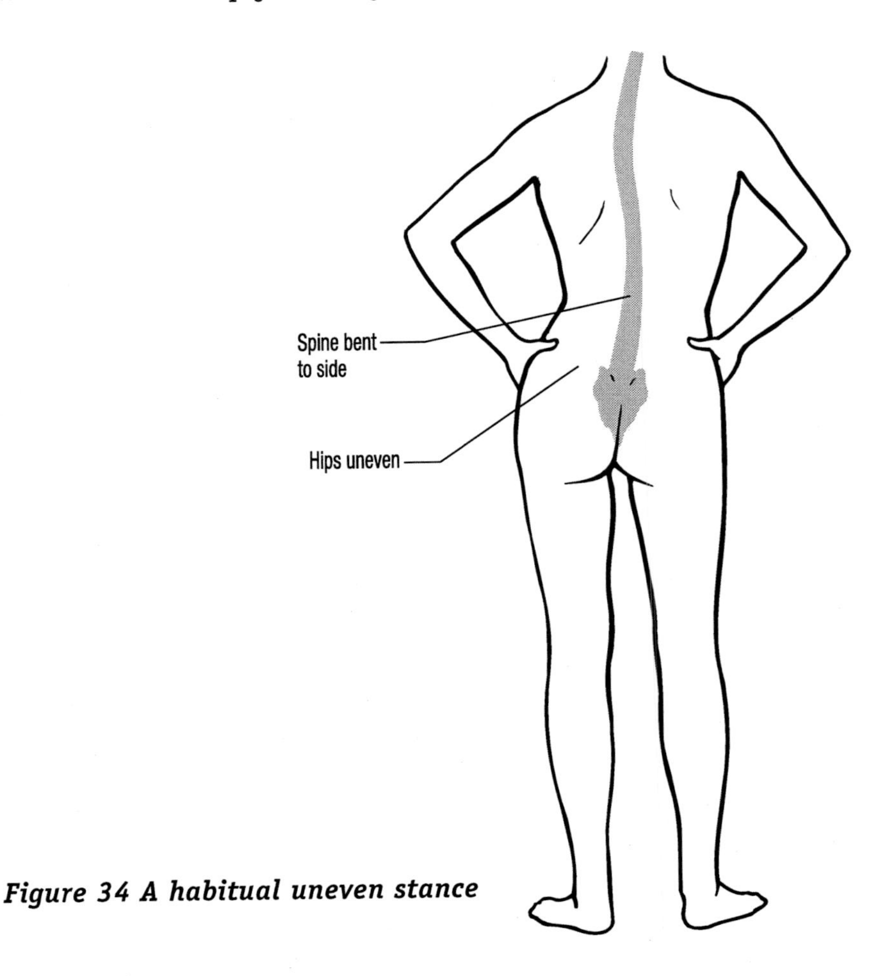


***Figure 34 A habitual uneven stance***

## Shoes

For the good of your feet and your back, shoes should be a good fit and comfortable, supporting the natural arches of your feet. Women's high heeled shoes do **not** fit this description! If a shoe raises your heel considerably higher than the ball of your foot this leads to complex changes in your legs, hips and lower back (*see figure* 35) changing your spinal posture.

- **Your ankle is stretched at the front.**
- **The knee is slightly bent.**
- **The hips are slightly bent.**
- **The lower back arches as the hips are thrown forward.**

A good insole, such as sorbethane, helps to absorb shocks – very useful if you walk on pavements a lot. A good grip on the sole helps to avoid accidents.

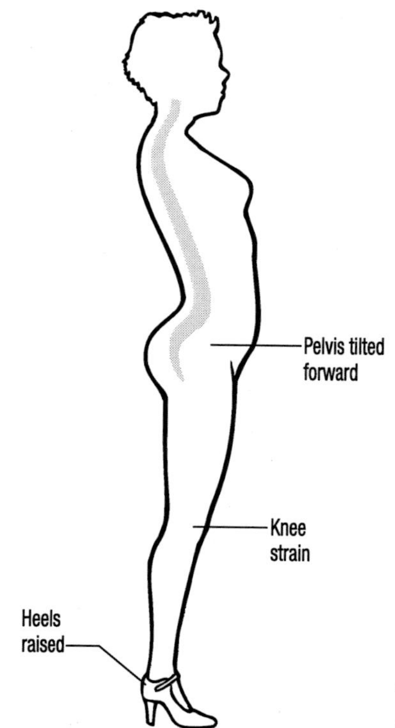


***Figure 35 Bad posture caused by high heels***

Anyone wearing high heeled shoes frequently is asking for low back problems. Remember, it may not hurt you now but it is making it more likely that you will suffer back pain at some time! *See also Standing at Kitchen Units/Sink page 132.*

## Sitting

'Right angles' are the key to good sitting. You should have right angles (90 degrees) at your ankles, knees, hips and elbows. Your seat must be designed in such a way as to support you in this position – if the seat forces you into a different position (e.g. a typical car seat) then you need to use cushions and towels to change the support the seat gives you – or just buy a new chair. There are various seating aids available that help you to modify your seat to achieve the support required (*see figure* 38).

***Figure 36 Bad seated posture***

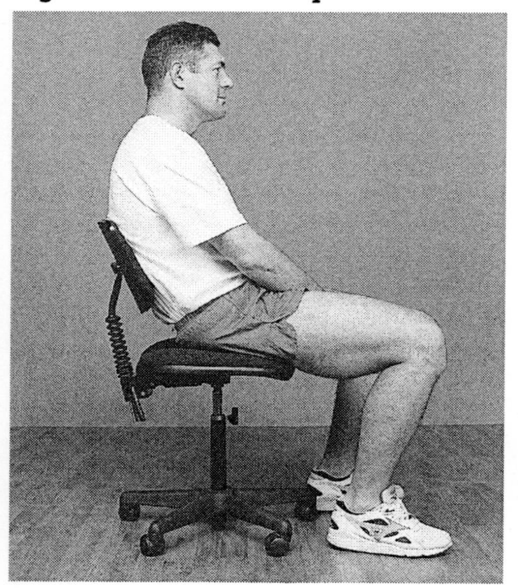

***Bottom too far forward***
***Poor support for lumbar spine***
***Ankle over-flexed, feet not resting flat on floor***
***Pressure on back of thigh***

***Good seated posture***

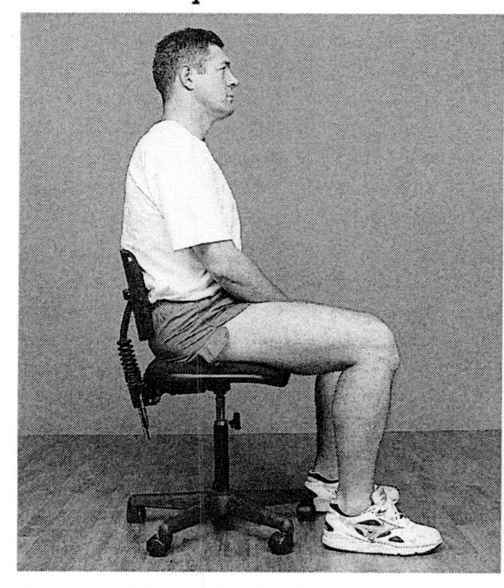

***Bottom right to back of seat***
***Good support in small of back***
***Ninety degree angle at ankle***

***Ninety degree angle at knee***

*Figure 37 Bad car seat posture* | *Good car seat posture*

*Knees higher than bottom*
*Lumbar spine rounded/flexed*
*Reaching for wheel*
*Rounded shoulders*

*Chin forward*

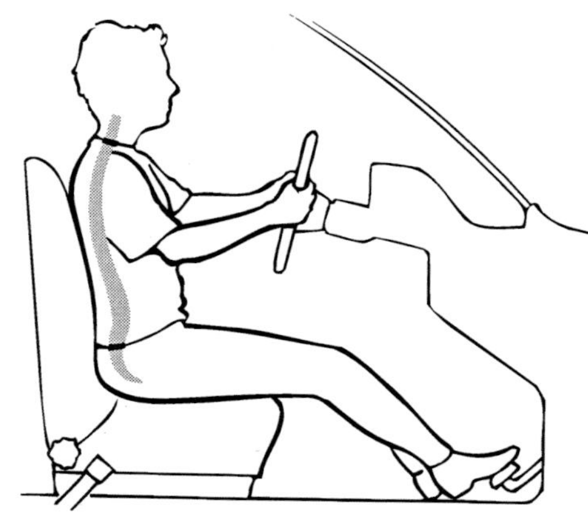

*Bottom as high as knees*
*Lumbar spine held in curve*
*Easy reach for wheel*
*Shoulders resting back on seat*
*Chin down*

If your job involves a lot of sitting or you have a hobby that is very sedentary (like watching TV!), it is very important that you ensure your sitting posture is as good as possible. Otherwise you will be putting stresses on your back (and other bits) that could be avoided. It is worth paying attention to anything that you do a lot. Do not believe that just because you are at rest you could not possibly be doing your back any harm. This is particularly true of sitting – you greatly increase the load on your lower back and most of its tissues when you sit.

**The bottom disc in your lower back is under approximately three times the pressure sitting as it is when you are standing!**

Sitting has great potential to do damage to your lower back – so make sure you get it right. There will be times when you just want to stretch out and lie back on a settee/sofa – as long as your back is well looked after most of the time, this will do you no harm at all. But if you regularly abuse your back this could be the last straw!

The kneeling chair is a type of seat that encourages your lower back to adopt its natural curve. The bottom support is tilted down at the front and there are pads to support your knees. This arrangement puts your pelvis and lower back in a position very similar to what it would be standing and this decreases the strain on your lower back. However, it comes at a price – there is no lumbar support to lean back on. Many people find that their lower back muscles tire quickly due to this lack of support. However, it is a good idea and one worth trying – you may find it tremendously useful. Many office/typist chairs have a function where the bottom support can be tilted down at the front and locked in this position. However, you then have to put one foot in front of the other to ensure you do not slip off the chair. Again though, this is probably worth experimenting with. *See Standing Up From A Chair page 134.*

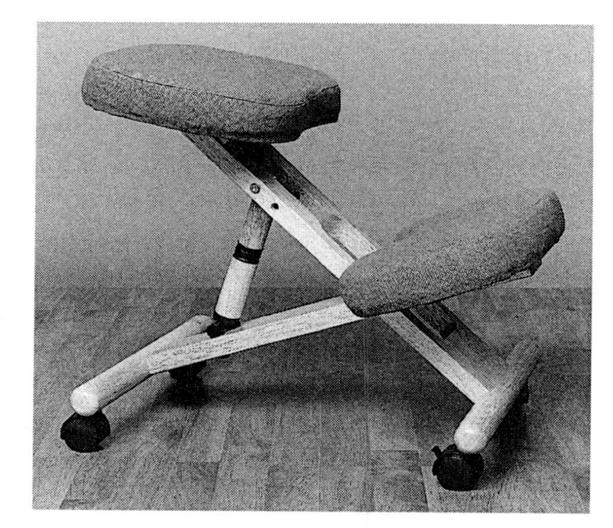

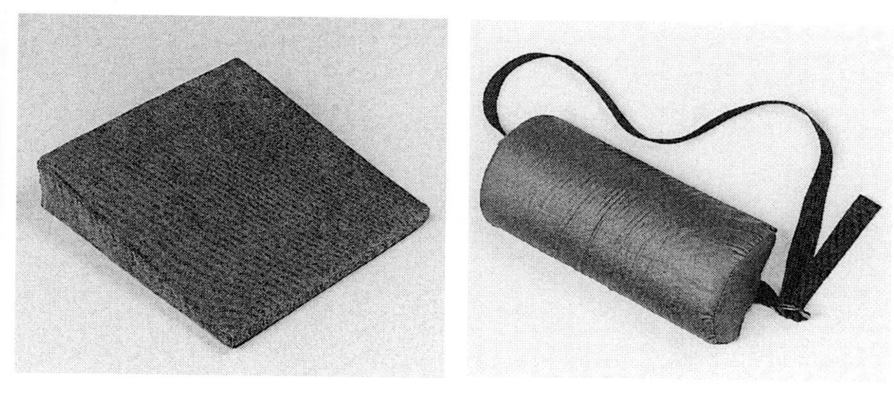

***Figure 38 A seat wedge and a lumbar roll***

## Lying

When lying down you should be in a position in which the natural curves in your spine are supported by whatever you are lying on. The curves should not be allowed to sag or be forced into exaggerated positions – this leads to stretching of ligaments and you wake up in the morning stiff and sore due to protective muscle tightness.

So, you should lie on something that helps to support you in a correct position. For most people this is a firm mattress – *see page 84* for instructions on how to find the right mattress. The mattress is there to support you, to hold all your curves, and this should be comfortable. If you lie on too hard a surface, for example, the floor, your curves will not be supported: the hollow bits have no support. If you lie on too soft a surface, your heavy bits sink in too much and your back bends. So, the mattress should fill the hollows in your back (or side) and support the other bits.

*Figure 39 Good and bad supine posture*

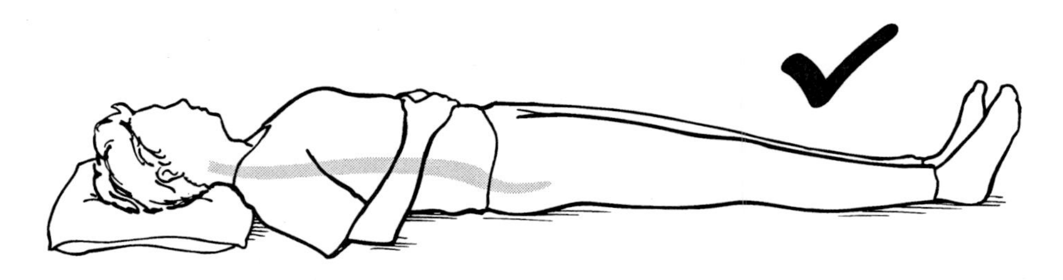

***Good supine posture***
***Lumbar spine relaxed and supported by mattress***
***Neck relaxed and supported by pillow***
***Body's natural curves supported***

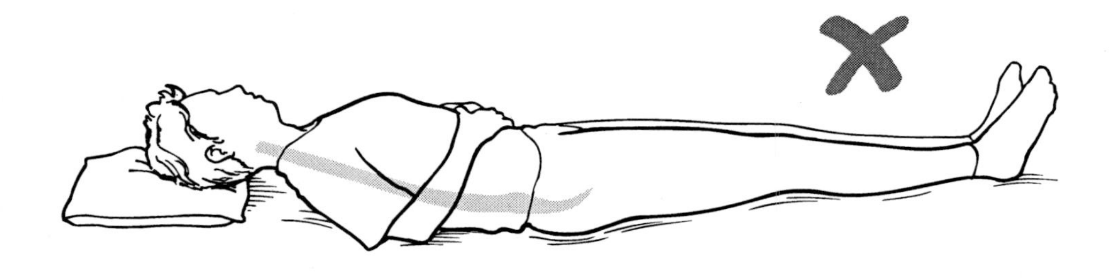

***Bad supine posture***
***Lumbar spine flexed and strained***
***Neck flexed and strained***
***Not accommodating body's curves***

Generally, lying on your front (prone) is not a good idea*. When lying prone you have to turn your head to one side in order to breathe freely and so that you don't squash your nose. This means that your neck will be twisted quite considerably for the whole time you are on your front. Although you may turn your head from side to side during this time, the fact is that either way you are stressing the tissues of your neck. Often in lying on your front you also allow your lower back to arch down towards

*Figure 40 Good and bad sidelying posture*

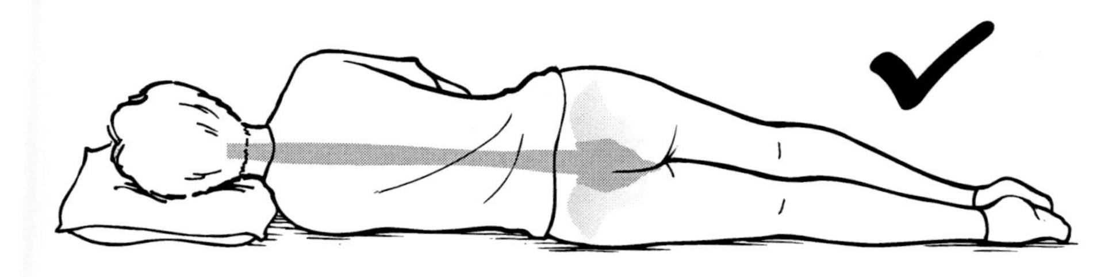

***Good sidelying posture***
***Spine held in straight line by mattress/pillows***
***Pelvis square due to support of upper thigh***

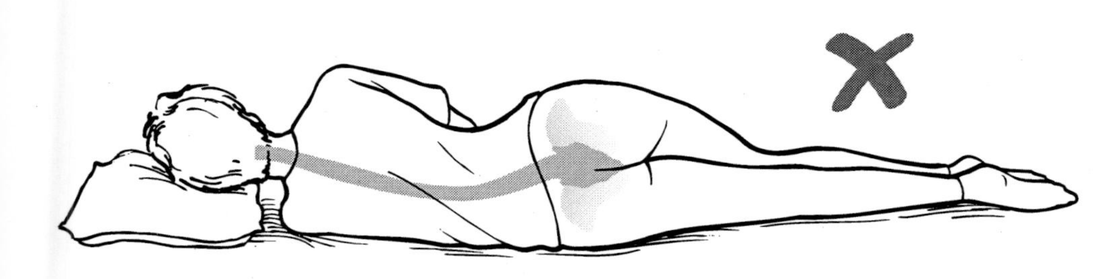

***Bad sidelying posture***
***Spine bent to side***
***Pelvis twisted***

the floor and this can lead to low back pain as the tissues here feel the strain.

*Some people with particular back problems find lying prone gives them some relief from their pain – discuss this with your chiropractor, osteopath or physiotherapist. *See Getting Up From Side Lying page 6.*

- **Lie on your back on the mattress.**
- **Put your hand in under the small of your back. If there is a gap between the mattress and your back then the mattress is too hard. If your back is rounding as it would in a hammock then the mattress is too soft.**
- **Lie on your side on the mattress, with a pillow supporting your head and neck.**
- **Get someone to look at the curves of your spine. Your spine should be in a fairly straight line when viewed from the back – not dipping too much towards the floor. Bear in mind that if your hips are much wider than your waist then your lower spine is bound to dip down towards the floor. If this is a problem you may need to support your side with a pillow –** ***see over.***

When buying a mattress, once you've found the right degree of firmness for you, bear in mind that you get what you pay for. A cheap mattress will probably lose its firmness faster than a more expensive one. It could be a false economy, if it means you have to replace the mattress more frequently and spend more on osteopath's fees! You can even lie on some cushions or a folded duvet on the floor – just so long as you're well supported and comfortable.

The waterbed has gone out of fashion since its popularity in the 1970s and '80s. However, a good waterbed can support your spine very well. The downside is that they can be quite expensive. Ideally, you should try one out before you buy one. They can present good support without pressurizing any one point greatly and are particularly suitable for elderly people.

## PILLOWS

Pillows are there to support your head and neck. Again, the important thing is that your normal spinal curves are maintained. When lying on your back, propping your head up too high will aggravate your lower back, and if your neck arches back too much this can also strain the lower back as it's difficult to relax. If you're lying on your side, your pillows should be thick enough to keep your head and neck horizontal – not pushed up or dropping down.

You can use pillows in other ways:

- **A pillow under the knees when you're on your back is often more comfortable than lying flat out.**
- **A pillow between your knees when you're on your side will often keep your top leg from slipping forwards and twisting your lower back painfully.**
- **A small pillow (or folded towel) around your waist when lying in bed can make things more comfortable – whether you're on your side or back.**

You can buy pillows ('orthopaedic pillows') which are shaped to support the curves of your neck. They fill the hollow of your neck and support this while also supporting your head. These are a good idea in principal. However, finding one the right size for you might prove difficult. As mentioned above the pillow should fill the hollow of your neck (whether lying on your back or your side).

***Figure 41 An orthopaedic pillow***

Sometimes a good feather pillow is the best at doing this job. If you are keen on an orthopaedic pillow try a friend's or see if the company will give you your money back if it turns out to be wrong for you.

You might try rolling up a towel, sellotaping it in this roll and putting it inside your pillowcase at the base of the pillow so that it creates a ridge to support your neck – it can prove difficult to keep the towel in place (try a tighter pillow case), but many people find this the best and cheapest solution. Experiment with the thickness, but as a rough guide, roll the towel up to the thickness of the middle of your forearm

Some people may have other factors to consider when trying to find the best posture for them. For example, if you suffer from heart problems it may be that lying flat for more than a short while is out of the question – consult your chiropractor, osteopath or physiotherapist for advice.

# Bad Exercise and Good Exercise

- The Importance of Exercise
- 'No Pain No Gain' – The Myth Exposed
- What Will the Exercises Achieve?
- General Exercise

## The Importance of Exercise

As we've said before 'Use it or Lose it but don't ever Abuse it'! If you're a chronic back pain sufferer you've already lost something (flexibility, strength or endurance) which has led you to this point. If you don't exercise, your back will not recover totally. It is widely known that exercise is vital if you are to put your back pain behind you.

## 'No Pain No Gain' – The Myth Exposed

We explained in 'Myths Exposed' that if an exercise hurts it could be setting back your recovery. This is the difficult bit – what's pain and what's just hard work? Some of the exercises given in this book will be hard work – your back should feel tired afterwards (although for most people not for long). If your back is actually painful during or after having done an exercise then consult your chiropractor, osteopath or physiotherapist but do not give up on the whole exercise programme.

## What Will the Exercises Achieve?

There are three important points to consider when we look at how healthy your back is. They are all related.

- **Flexibility: if your back is not flexible (and this includes your hips) you are more likely to stretch something painfully.**
- **Strength: if your back is weak you will strain it all too easily.**
- **Endurance: if your back tires quickly, again you will strain it easily.**

So, exercises should achieve:

- **Good flexibility**
- **Good strength**
- **Good endurance**

*See Exercises for Chronic Back Pain Sufferers page 94.*

## General Exercise

However, remember not to aggravate your pain by attempting exercises that are beyond you at the moment. There are three excellent forms of exercise for general fitness.

**People who are generally fit suffer less back pain than people who are not!**

- ***Walking*. As mentioned earlier, build up the amount of walking gradually. You should walk briskly for at least half an hour to improve your general health.**
- ***Swimming*. Do not attempt this if you are not a competent swimmer. No point in struggling – it'll probably do your back more harm than good! There is no reason why you can't take**

swimming lessons when your back is stronger. Again, you should swim constantly for at least half an hour. Remember, if you swim on your front your face must go into the water. Do not swim with your head stuck up in the air (social breaststroke) – this could aggravate your lower back and cause all kinds of neck problems. Of all the strokes breaststroke is most likely to aggravate a back problem – try sculling on your back to start with.

➲ *Water aerobics (Aqua aerobics)* are also an excellent form of exercise, particularly for those people who are not good swimmers. Most swimming pools hold classes in aqua aerobics. There is no need to put your face in the water, although you are likely to splash your own face as you move around. As with swimming, the strain is removed from your joints and yet your muscles get a good workout. Sports people returning from injury often use water-based exercise as one of the stages of recovery.

Simply trying to walk through the water can be hard work, especially if you hold your hands with your palms open at your sides facing forwards – this makes your passage through the water that much harder. The faster you try to go the harder you'll find it.

Cycling is often worth a try too, although you may have to experiment with how high to have the saddle and the handlebars. Don't bend your back in leaning forwards onto the handlebars, try and keep your back fairly straight: *see figure 42*. Remember not to get carried away with cycling – no jarring! Wait until your back is stronger. It may be better to start on a stationary bike.

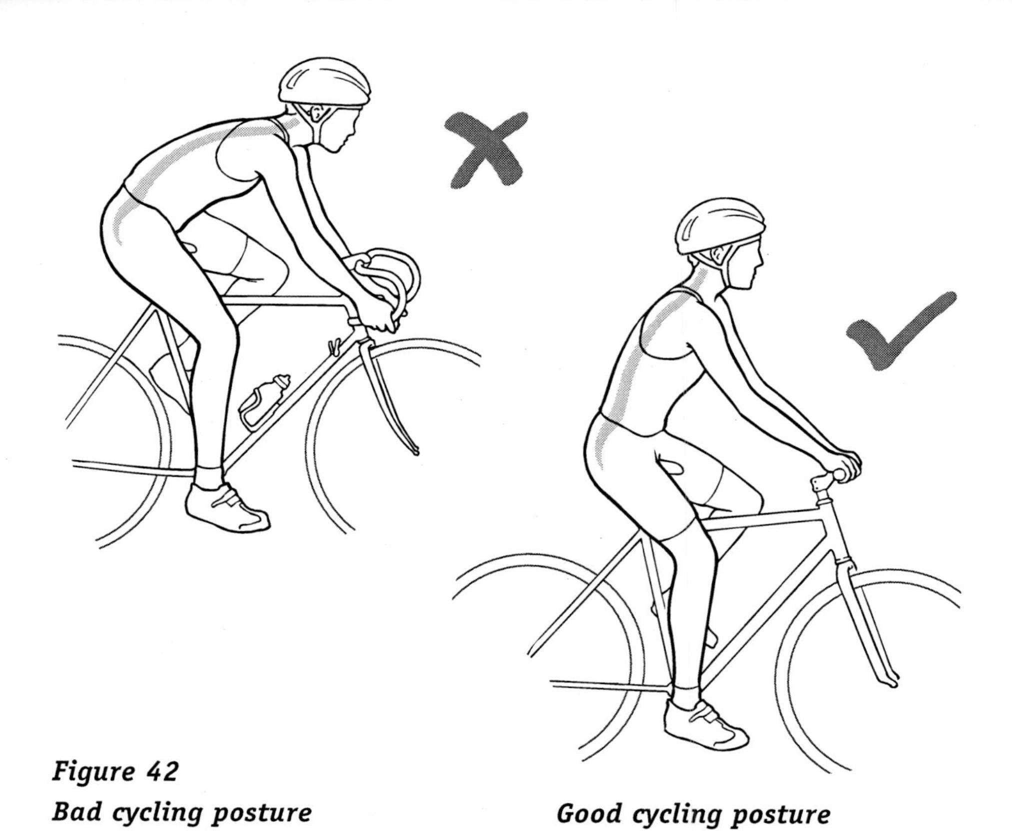

*Figure 42*
***Bad cycling posture***

***Good cycling posture***

# Bad Health and Good Health

- The Importance of Good Health
- Good Nutrition and Being Overweight
- Smoking
- Other Disabilities

## The Importance of Good Health

People who are generally fit and well suffer less disability from back pain than people who are generally unfit. Good health means being well in body and mind. You must find a balance between work and play, being well-nourished but not over-nourished (i.e. overweight), exercising but not over-exercising (to the edge of exhaustion).

- **Good health includes good circulation.**
- **Good circulation is essential for your body to heal well and for all the various support systems to work at their optimum level.**
- **Movement is essential to maintain your circulation – without it your blood and lymph (a fluid which bathes all your body's tissues and rejoins your blood circulation) stagnate and will not nourish your tissues as they should.**

## Good Nutrition and Being Overweight

You take in food to supply yourself with energy and nutrients (vitamins, minerals etc.) which are essential to allow your body's processes to work. If your diet is not a balanced one then you will not heal as quickly as you might with a better diet. However, this is not a diet book – *see Recommended Reading on page 155.*

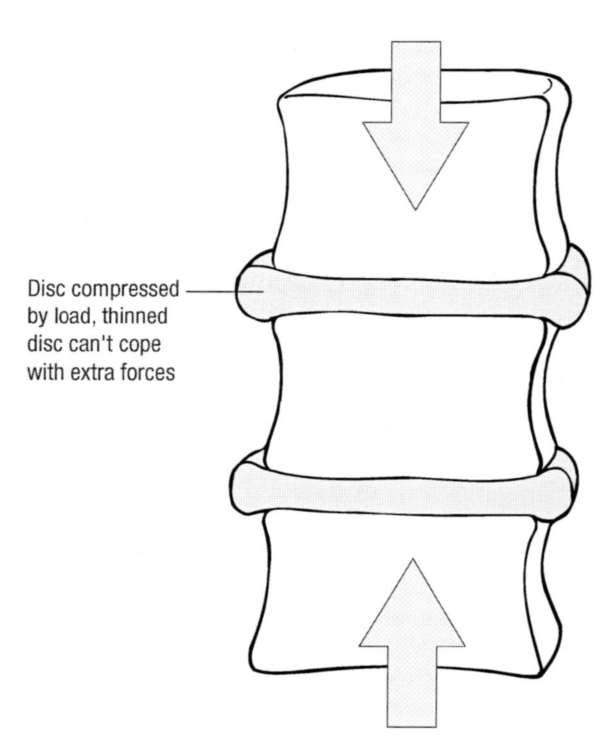


***Figure 43 How excess body weight affects your discs***

If you are overweight for your height you are carrying around a greater load than is advisable. This increases the strain on your lower back, making it harder for it to get better, and increasing the chance that something will go wrong again. The greater the weight bearing down on the bones and discs in your lower back, the more likely things (bones, discs, muscles) are to tire and wear out (*see figure* 45).

Again, this is not a diet book. But as being overweight could well be an aggravating factor for your low back pain, it is well worth trying to do something about this. We would advise you to read at least one of the books recommended on page 155. Remember, how **much** do you want to rid yourself of back pain?

## Smoking

No lecture here. Just the simple fact that:

**Smokers suffer more disability through back pain than non-smokers.**

## Other Disabilities

If you suffer from any chronic ongoing problem, it is likely that this has a very direct effect on your back. For example:

- **People who have a limp due to old polio and leg shortening put more of a strain on their lower back because their movements are not as smooth. One hip bone is higher than the other, placing a constant strain on the muscles, discs, bones and ligaments of the lower back.**
- **People who suffer digestive problems (e.g. irritable bowel syndrome, Crohn's Disease) may not be absorbing all the nutrients they need from their food and so they will not heal as quickly as someone with good bowel function.**
- **People who have a chronic heart condition often cannot lie flat for long, and in propping themselves up in bed exert a strain on the tissues of the lower back.**

So, you can see that all the above are aggravating factors in low back pain and this should be taken into account in setting your goals. It is recommended that anyone suffering similar problems in addition to their low back pain consult a chiropractor, osteopath or physiotherapist before undertaking the exercises and advice set out in this book.

# Exercises for Chronic Back Pain Sufferers

- What the Exercises Should Achieve
- When and Where You Should Do the Exercises
- What to Wear
- How Often To Do the Exercises
- When You Can Stop the Exercise Programme
- The Exercises
- Planning Your Exercise Programme

## What the Exercises Should Achieve

In this section of the book we present exercises recommended for those with ongoing back pain. After this we give some recommended programmes of exercises for general fitness aimed at those with chronic back pain. The exercises are aimed at improving your flexibility, strength and endurance, the importance of each of these was outlined previously.

We're not trying to make you into an Arnie Schwarzenеggar or Charles Atlas. Your back does not need to be super strong; just strong enough to cart you around, carry shopping, lift the baby out of the cot, etc. And you have to be able to do these things several times a day without your back tiring and causing pain. Strength need only be moderate, but your back needs to last. So, the exercises given here may prove to be very easy to do once or ten times, but to do a hundred times may be way beyond you for several months. But it's this gradual build up which will increase the endurance and flexibility of your back, so that it doesn't get tired and sore so easily – don't rush it.

## When and Where You Should Do the Exercises

- **The stretch exercises can be done just about any time, but should always be done after any strengthening exercises, and after any other exercise you take.**
- ***Don't* do the strengthening exercises on a full stomach.**
- ***Don't* do the strengthening exercises within half an hour of being in bed: wait until you've been up for at least half an hour, and don't do them within half an hour of going to bed.**
- **Preferably choose a time of day when you are feeling good – don't exercise when you are tired or depressed. You will soon give up on this!**
- **Make sure you choose a time when you will not be interrupted. This is perhaps the most important thing. Remember – if it's worth doing, it's worth doing right! Your main exercise activity of the day must be done on these terms. If you're just doing a little bit of stretching here and there, don't worry about being interrupted – you can make up for it later.**

You should exercise in an area that you feel comfortable in. It is best to have a well-ventilated room, with everything in it that you may need to make your exercising easier and more enjoyable. Some people like the distraction of music, for example. A foam mat on the floor is ideal. A bed is usually too soft for good exercising. Make sure you have plenty of room to stretch out in; that you are not worried about knocking things over! Wear something comfortable that's not going to restrict your movements to exercise in.

## How Often To Do the Exercises

The strengthening exercises should be done once a day, 6 days a week. The stretching exercises should be done every day, two to four times a day (depending on how stiff you are and how much time you can find to devote to getting better).

## When You Can Stop the Exercise Programme

Never! You will reach a point where you can cut back to twice or three times a week, but that is likely to be at least a year away (if you've suffered for at least a year). It will take a long time to strengthen your back and it is possible you will have small relapses of acute pain which will mean you have to stop the strengthening exercises for a while. Even when you've been pain free for a year do not take it for granted; keep doing the exercises that got you there and remember – how much does it mean to you?

## The Exercises

### *Flexibility*

Remember, if any of these exercises seem to aggravate your pain then don't do them or don't do them so vigorously. Consult your chiropractor, osteopath or physiotherapist if in any doubt.

## GLUTEAL/BUTTOCK STRETCH

1. Lying on your back raise one knee up towards your chest.
2. Gripping behind the knee pull the knee towards the opposite shoulder until you feel the tightness in your buttock.
3. Do not stretch beyond this tightness, but hold this point and relax for 10 seconds. (If you feel a tightness in the groin, do not go beyond this point.)
4. Lower the leg back down to rest straight out, and repeat with the other leg.
5. Always have the resting leg flat and straight on the floor.
6. Do this three times each side, alternating.

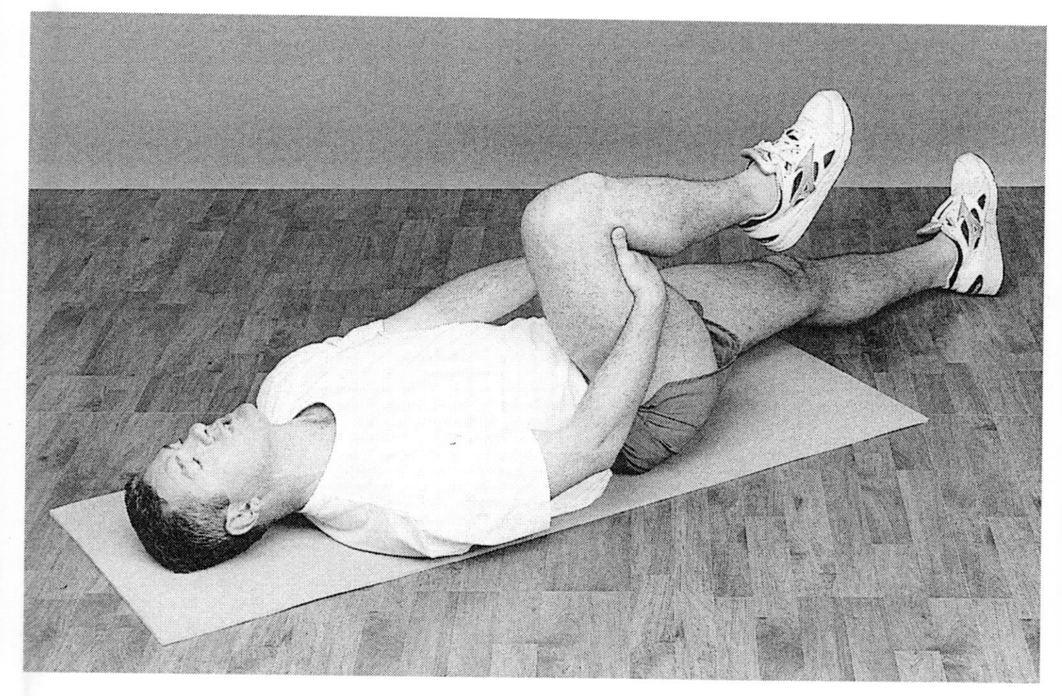

*Figure 44 Gluteal/Buttock stretch*

## STANDING GLUTEAL STRETCH

1. Rest the outside of one ankle on a table or tall stool.
2. Bend the supporting leg at the knee, keeping your back straight.
3. Lower yourself down gradually on this leg until you feel the stretch in the buttock. (If your supporting leg is weak it will be an effort to support yourself on it!)

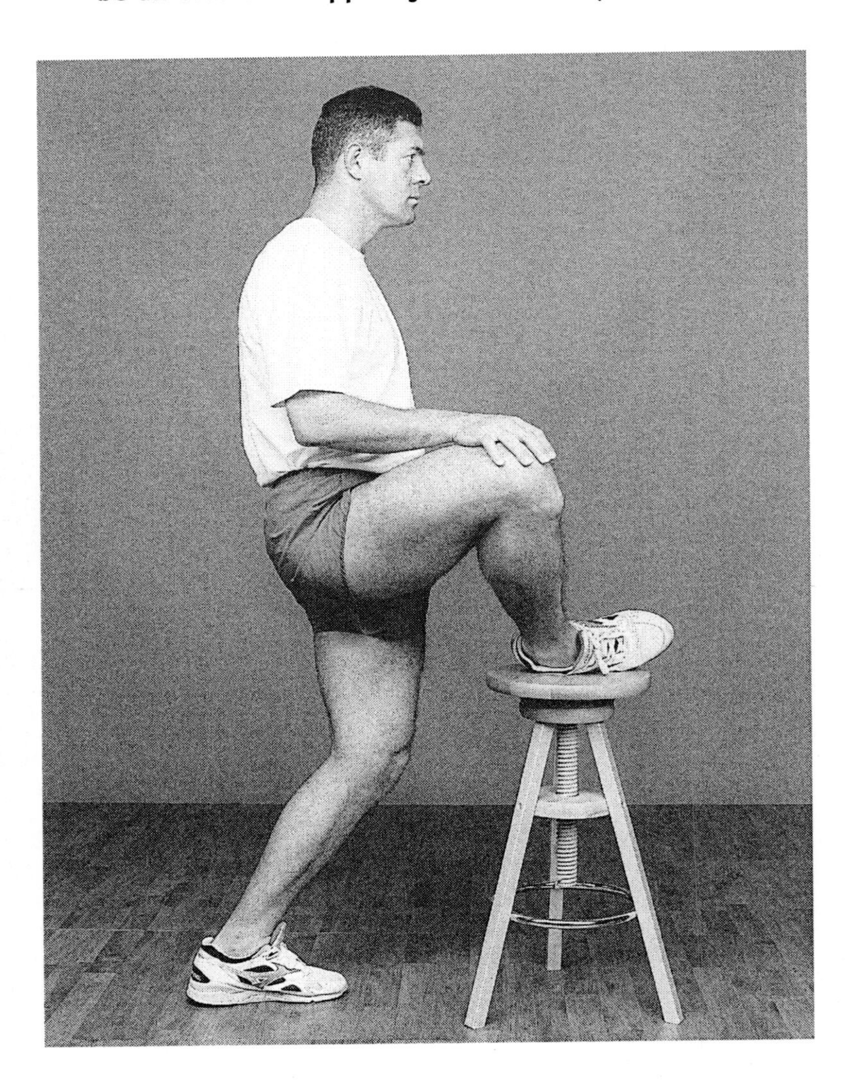

*Figure 45 Standing gluteal stretch*

## CRUCIFIX

1 Lying on your back, bend both knees up, feet flat on the floor.
2 Shift your hips to one side a little.
3 Allow your knees to fall to the opposite side, keeping your shoulders flat on the floor.
4 You may feel a stretch down the uppermost side/buttock area.
5 Do not force your knees over, but hold this point and relax for 30 seconds.
6 Repeat the same manoeuvre to the opposite side, shifting your hips first.
7 Do this twice each side, alternating.

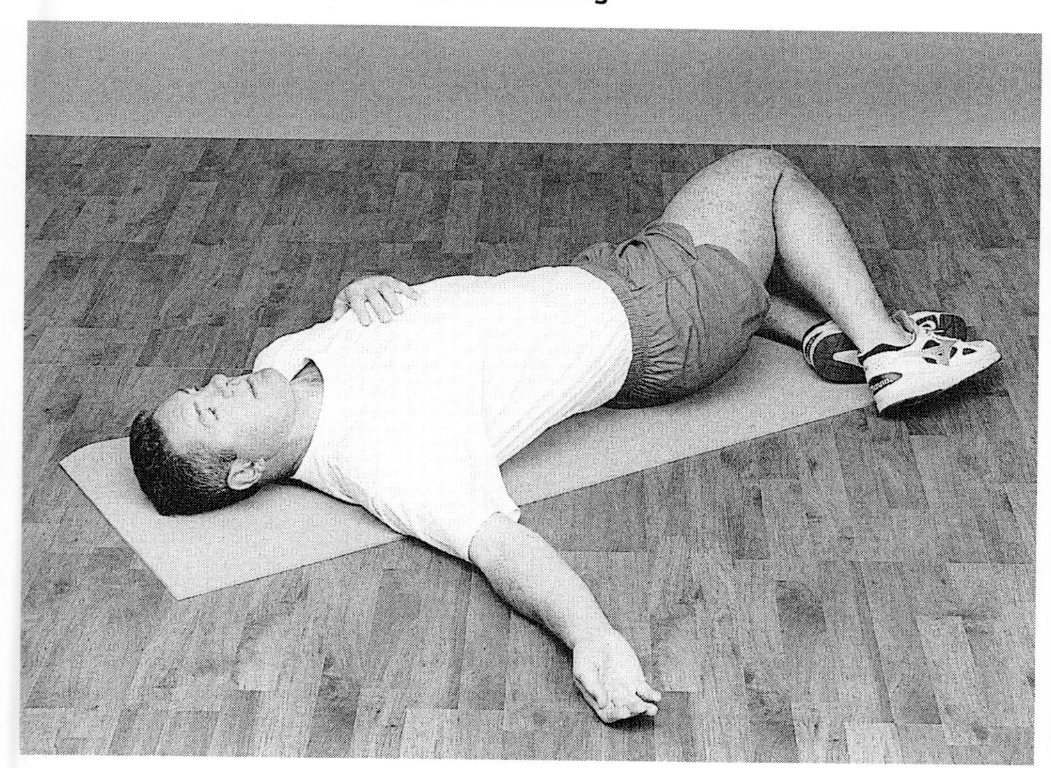

*Figure 46 Crucifix*

## LUMBAR FLEXION

1. Lie on your back with your knees bent up.
2. Pull one knee up and grab hold of it, then pull the other knee up and grab hold of it so that you are gripping the back of both knees, gently pulling towards your chest.
3. In this position, very slightly rock your knees backwards and forwards so that you feel a gentle stretch at the base of your back. No pain!
4. Rock for 30 seconds.

*Figure 47 Lumbar flexion*

## LUMBAR EXTENSION

1. Lie face down, leaning on your elbows.
2. Arch the small of your back to press your pelvis and stomach to the floor.
3. Try and relax in this position for 30 seconds (or for up to 2 minutes if it relieves your pain).

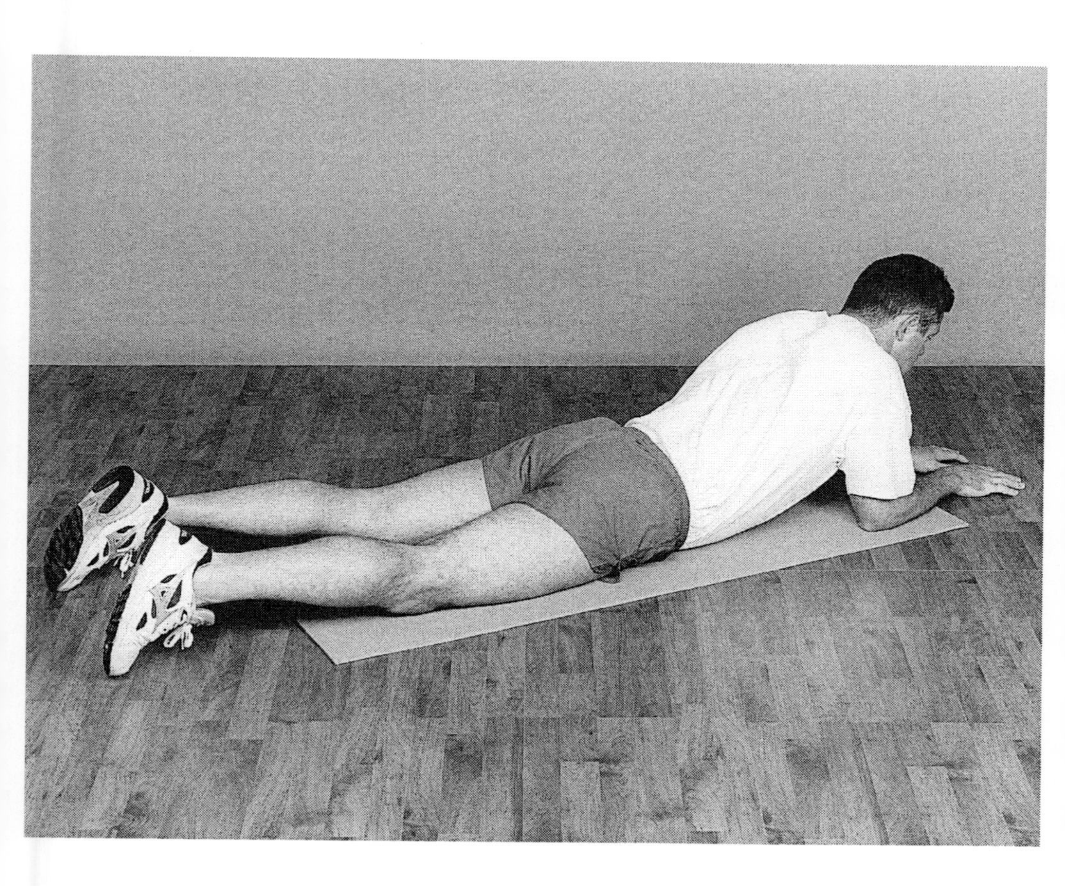

*Figure 48 Lumbar extension*

## STANDING LUMBAR EXTENSION

1. Stand with your feet shoulder width apart.
2. Put your hands on the back of your hips.
3. Arch your back backwards.
4. Hold for 3 seconds.

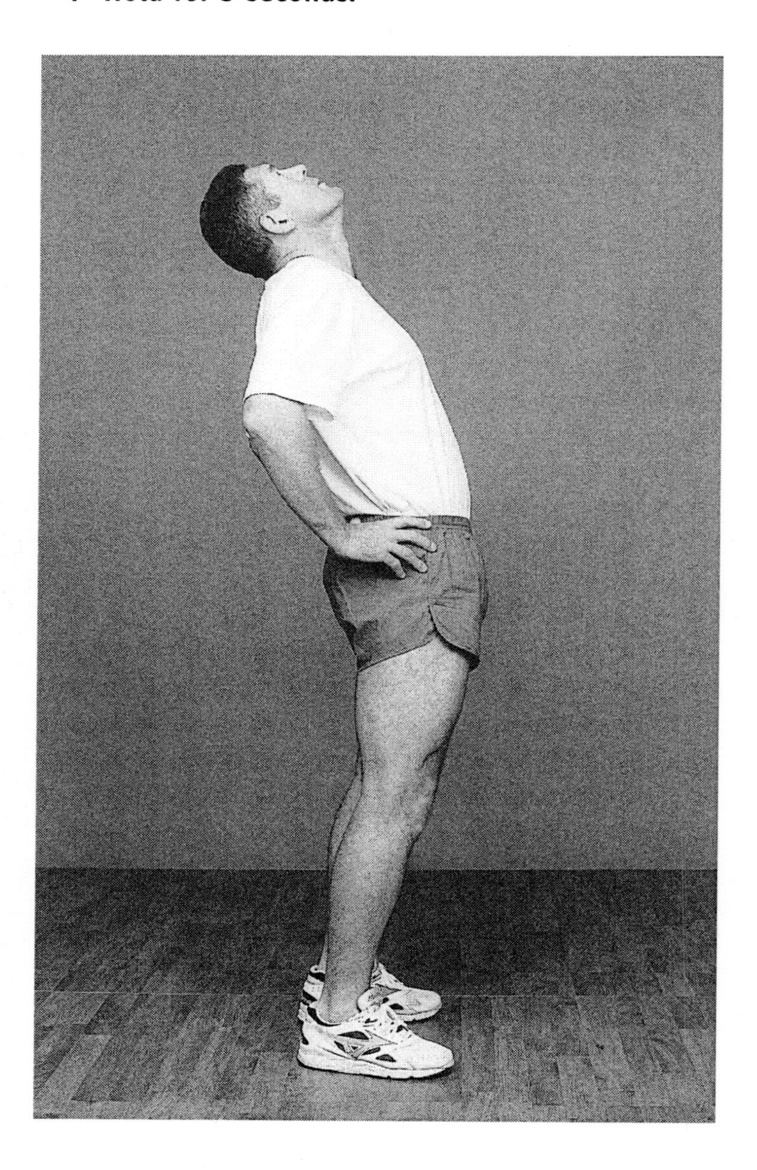

*Figure 49 Standing lumbar extension*

## HAMSTRING STRETCH

1 Lie on your back with both legs straight out.
2 Bend one knee up and grab the back of your thigh.
3 Without lifting your head, slowly try to straighten the knee until you feel the stretch in the back of your thigh/leg – do not go beyond this point. No pain!
4 Hold this stretch for 10 seconds.
5 Repeat on alternate sides, six times in total.

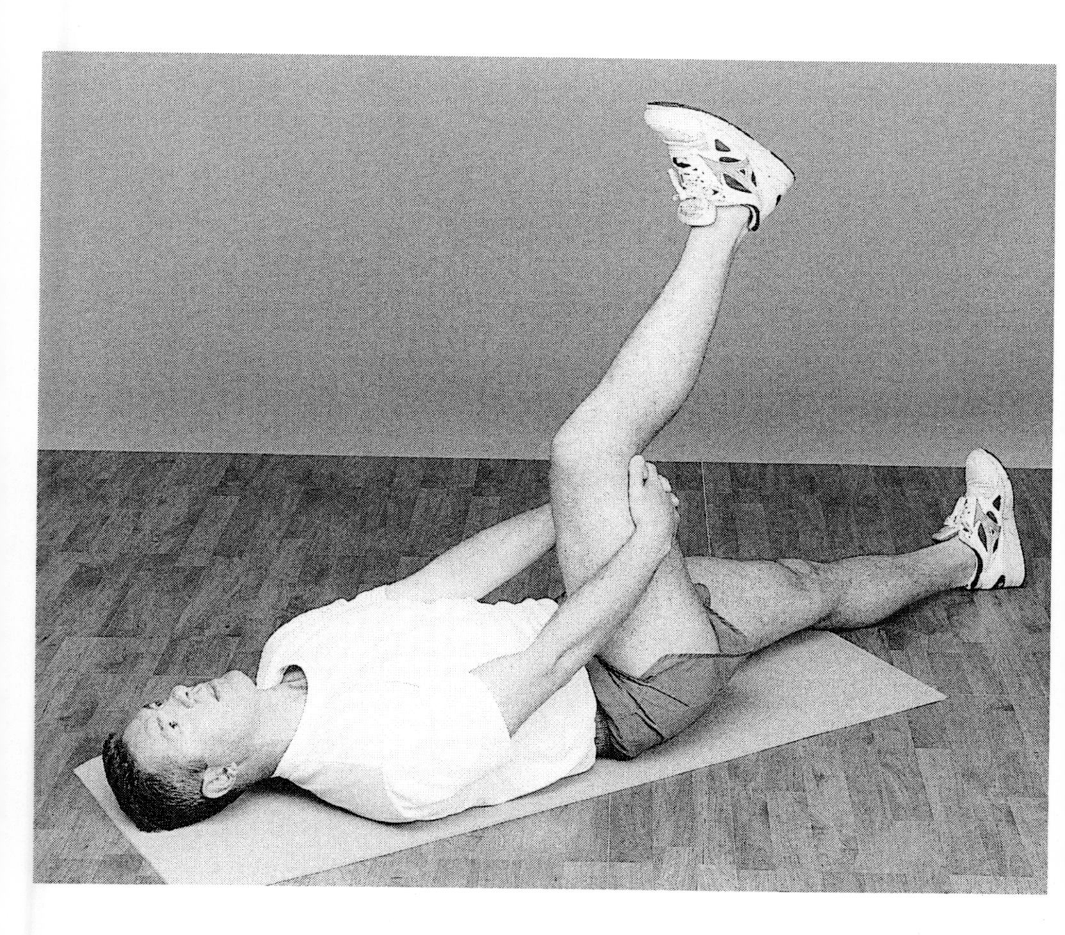

*Figure 50 Hamstring stretch*

## STANDING HAMSTRING STRETCH

1. Support your weight on one leg, putting the other out in front of you, resting on the heel.
2. Bend the supporting leg at the knee, putting both hands on this thigh.
3. Stretch the toes of the front leg up towards you.
4. Feel the stretch at the back of the thigh/knee on the front leg (if the supporting leg is weak this exercise will be quite an effort).
5. Do not bend your back forwards.
6. Hold for 10 seconds.

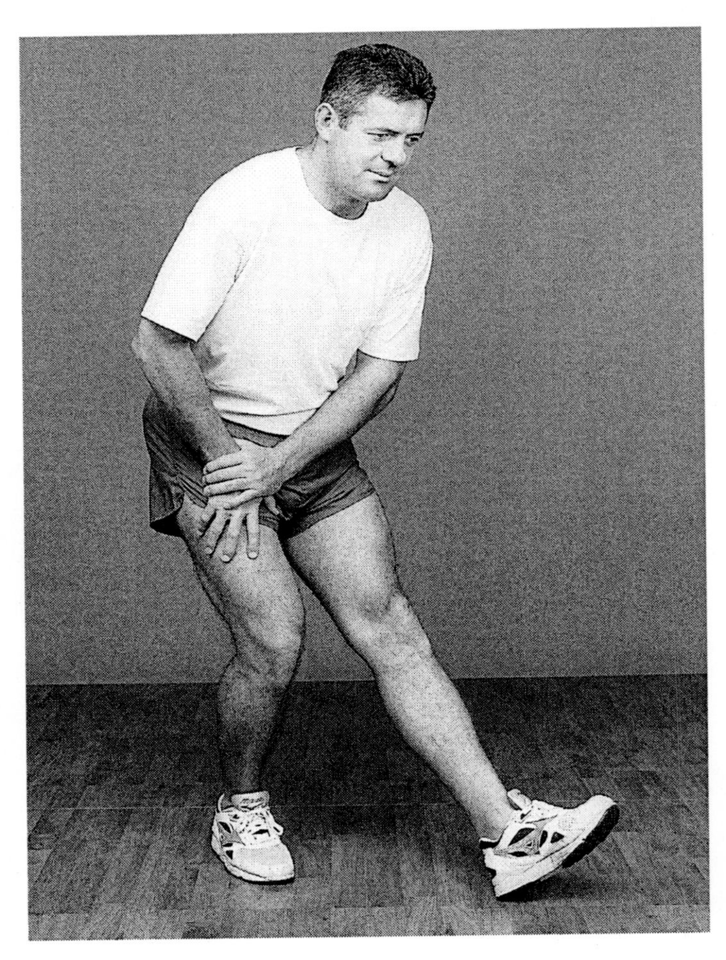

*Figure 51 Standing hamstring stretch*

## ADDUCTOR STRETCH

1 Stand with your feet approximately 3 feet apart, facing forwards.
2 Bring your weight over to one side, bending the knee on that side.
3 Keep the other knee straight.
4 Feel the stretch on the inside of the straight thigh.
5 Hold for 10 seconds.

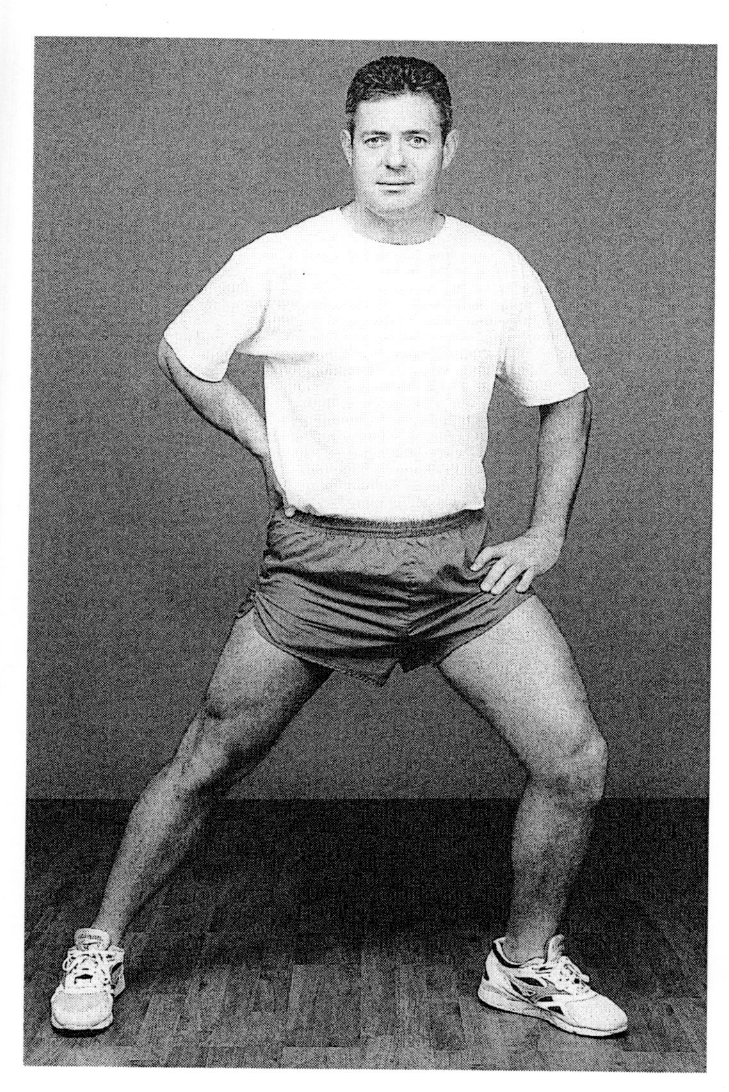

*Figure 52 Adductor stretch*

## QUADRICEPS STRETCH

1 Stand holding on to a support with one hand.
2 With the other hand, pull your ankle up towards your bottom.
3 Keep your knees together.
4 Feel the stretch down the front of your thigh.
5 Hold this stretch for 10 seconds.
6 Repeat on alternate sides three times.

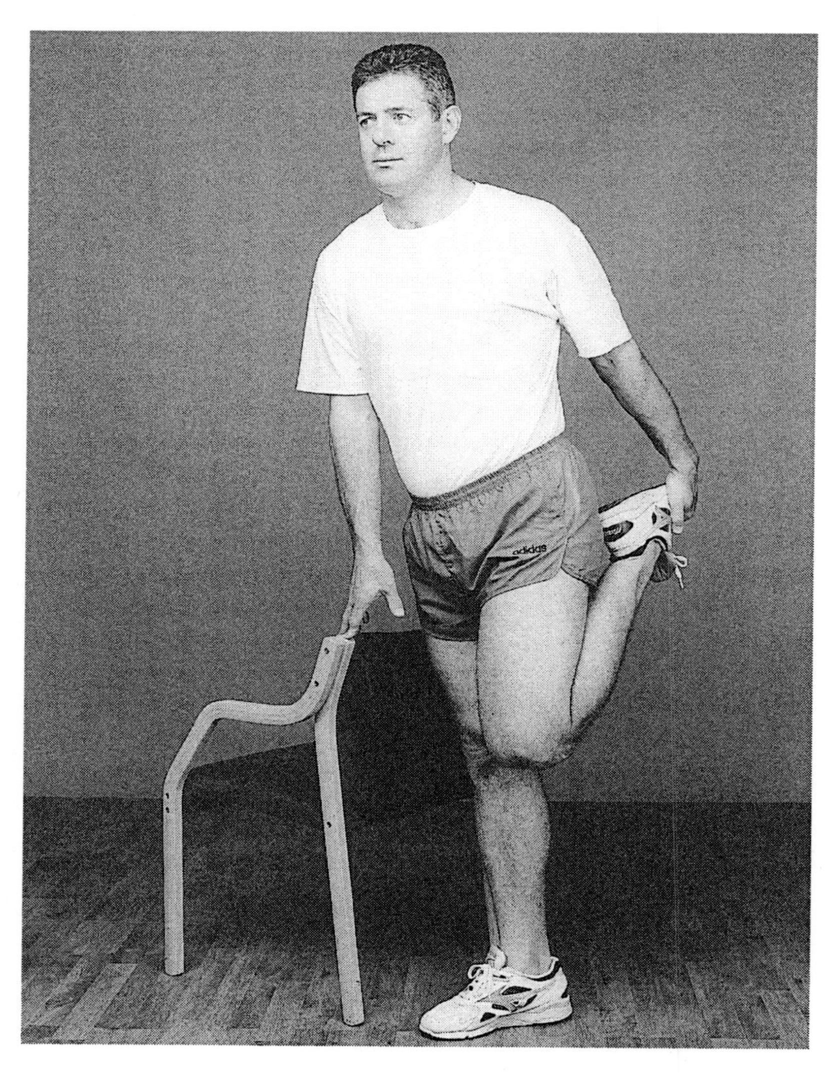


*Figure 53 Quadriceps stretch*

## CALF STRETCH

1 Put one foot approximately 3 feet in front of the other, both feet facing forwards.
2 Bring your weight forward onto the front leg, bending the knee.
3 Keep the heel of the back foot on the floor.
4 You may find it easier to lean against a wall.
5 Hold this position for 10 seconds.

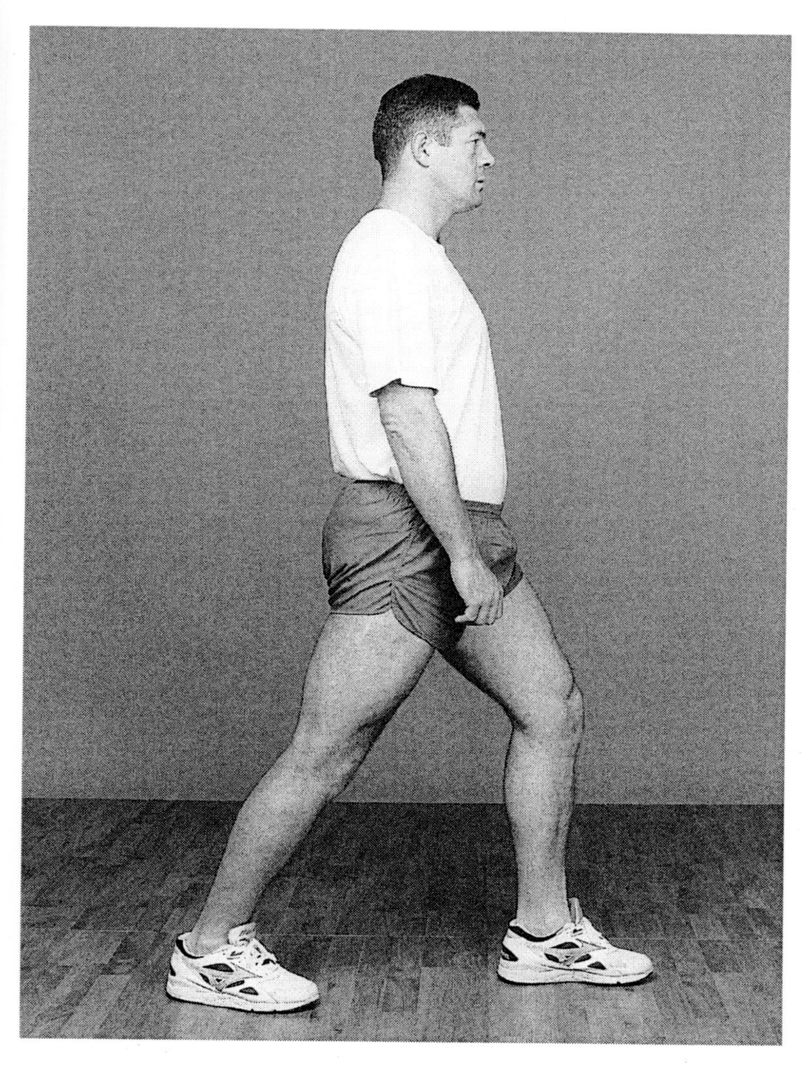

*Figure 54 Calf stretch*

## PSOAS STRETCH

1. Lie face down on a table with one leg on the floor and a cushion under the supported knee.
2. Bend the knee on the table and pull your heel towards your bottom with your hand.
3. If you cannot feel a stretch, then lift your shoulder up on the same side.
4. Hold for 20 seconds.

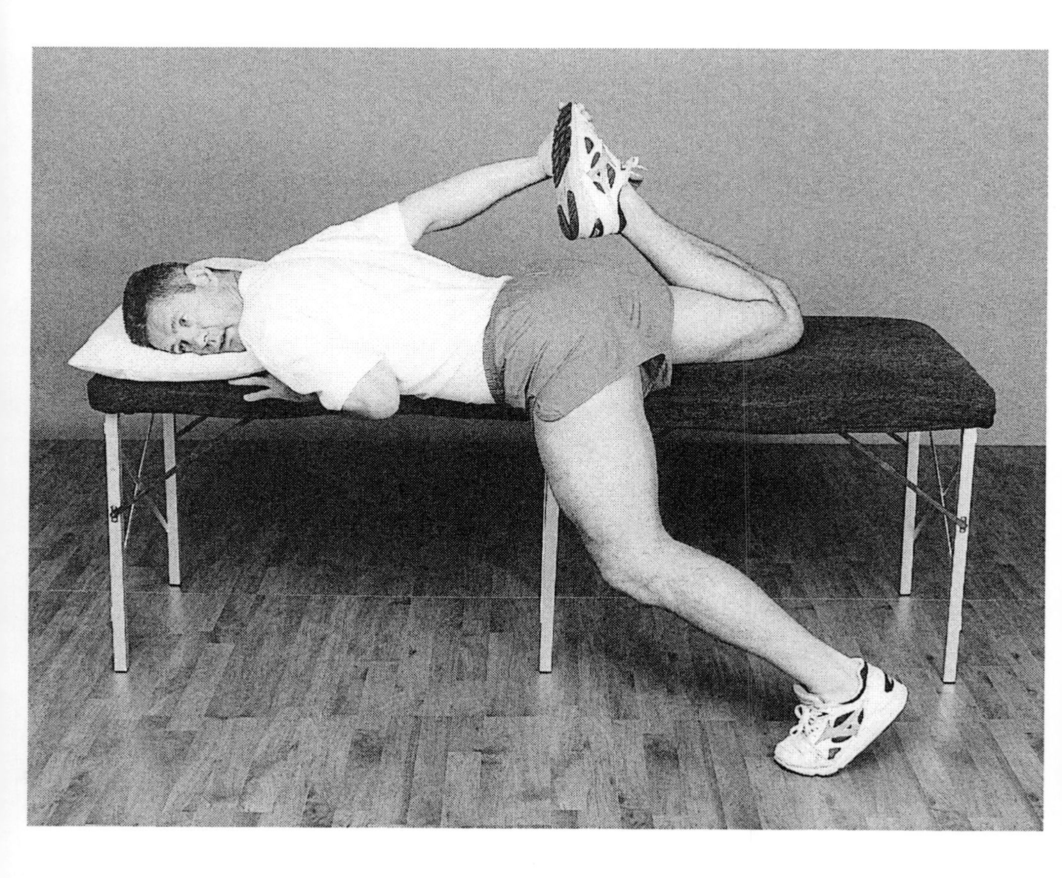

*Figure 55a Psoas stretch*

**alternatively:**

1. **Lie on your back on a table with the lower halves of your legs dangling off the end.**
2. **Lift one knee up towards the chest and hold the back of your thigh.**
3. **Relax for 20 seconds, feeling the stretch at the front of the hanging leg.**
4. **Pull the hanging leg up and grab hold of it before relaxing the other leg so that it hangs down.**

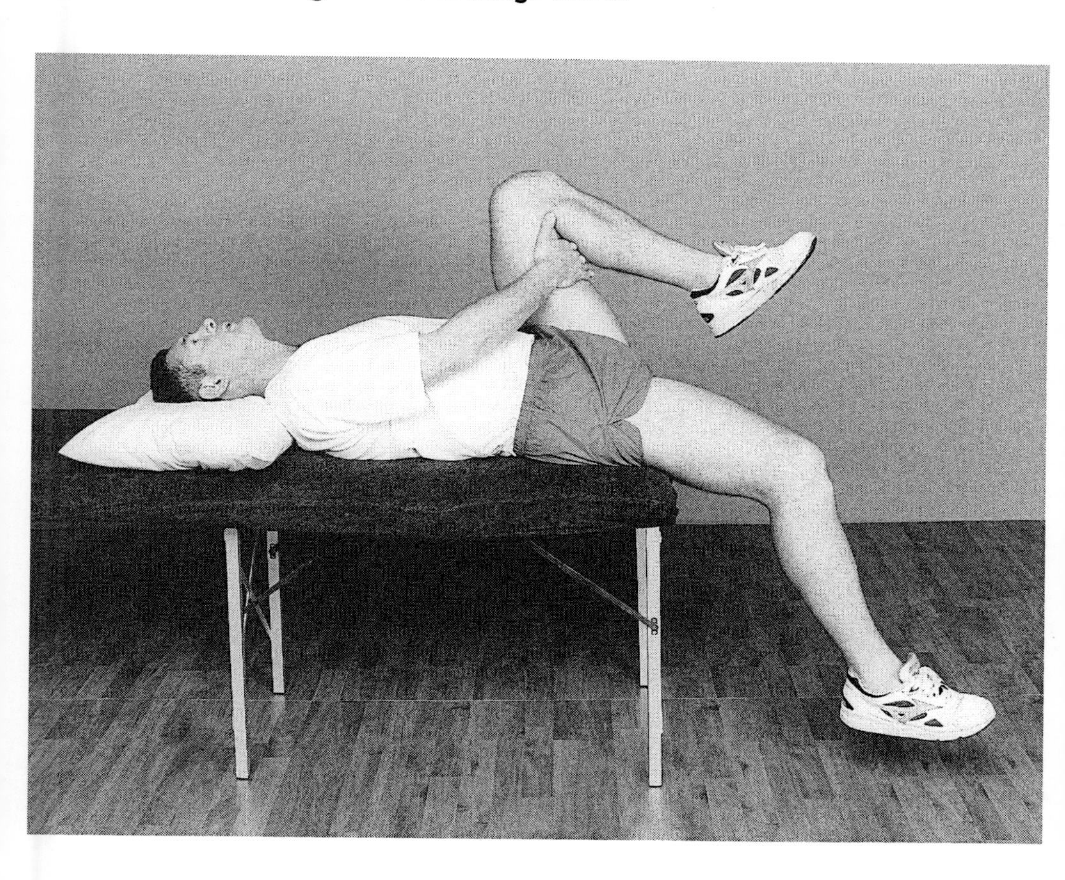

*Figure 55b Psoas stretch*

## STANDING SIDEBENDING STRETCH

1 Stand with your feet approximately 2 feet apart.
2 Bend over to one side (don't go forwards or backwards).
3 If necessary, support your trunk by putting your hand on the thigh you are bending towards.
4 Bring the other arm over or behind your head.
5 Feel the stretch down your side.
6 Hold for 10 seconds.

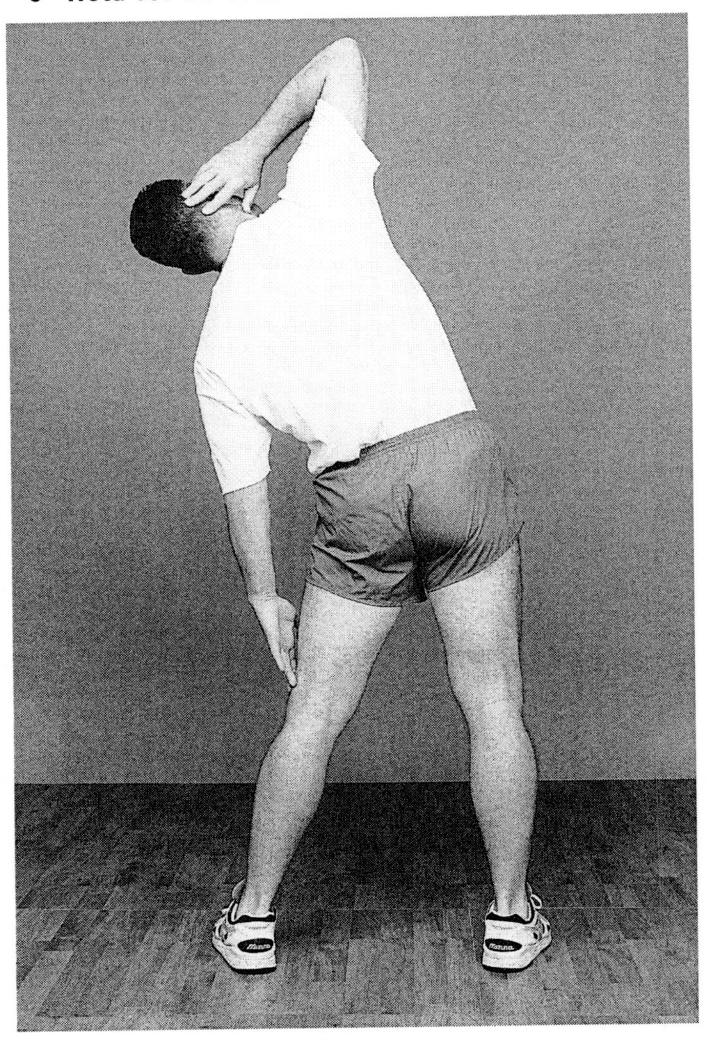

*Figure 56 Standing sidebending stretch*

## SITTING ROTATION

1 Sit in a chair with your knees facing forwards.
2 Twist to one side, holding onto the chair back.
3 Hold for 5 seconds.

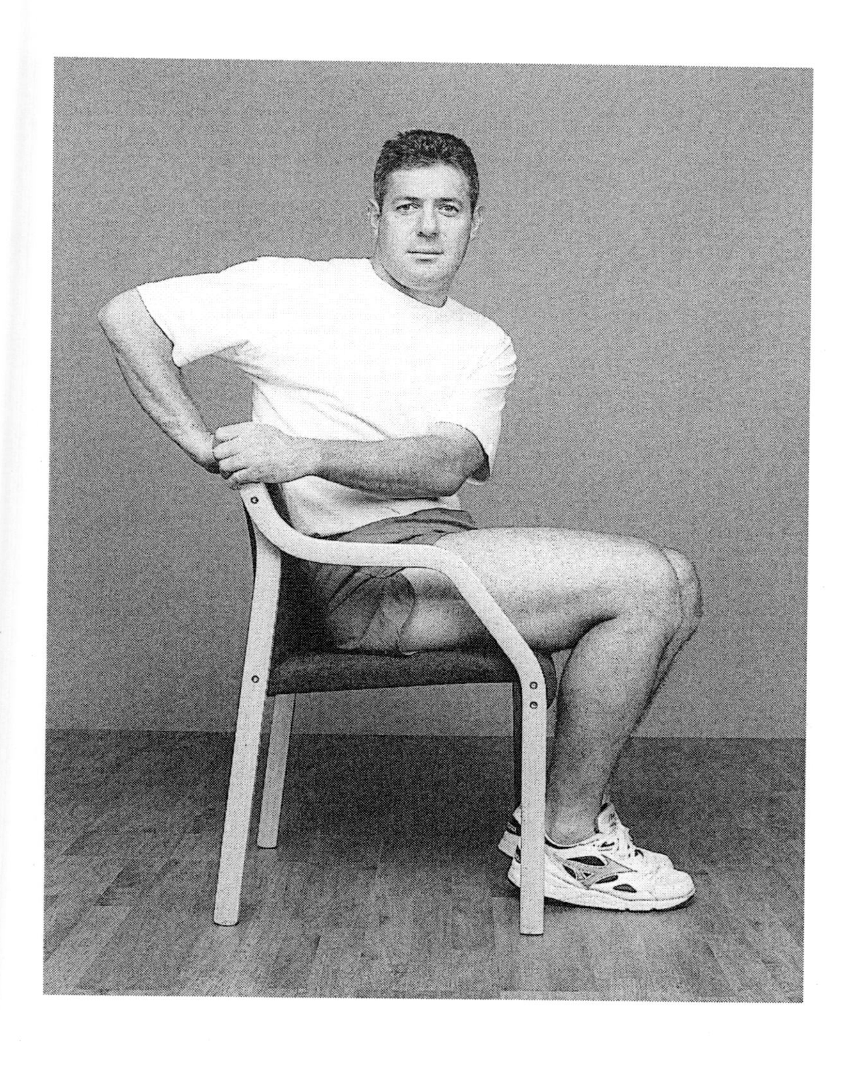

*Figure 57 Sitting rotation*

## *Strength/Endurance Exercises*

### ABDOMINALS AND PELVIC TUCK

1. Lie on your back with both knees bent up, feet flat on the floor.
2. Reach with your hands to touch the fronts of your thighs.
3. Keep your chin pointing towards your knees, do not pull it into your chest.
4. Lift your shoulders and head up slightly until you feel your stomach muscles tighten.
5. Reach with your hands to touch your knees. Do not come up any higher.
6. Relax back down, coming back up before reaching a point of rest.
7. Repeat 10–50 times (if you feel light-headed, stop and rest).

N.B. Some people find this very hard to do – take advice from your chiropractor, osteopath or physiotherapist. Some people find it very easy to do – do more of them!

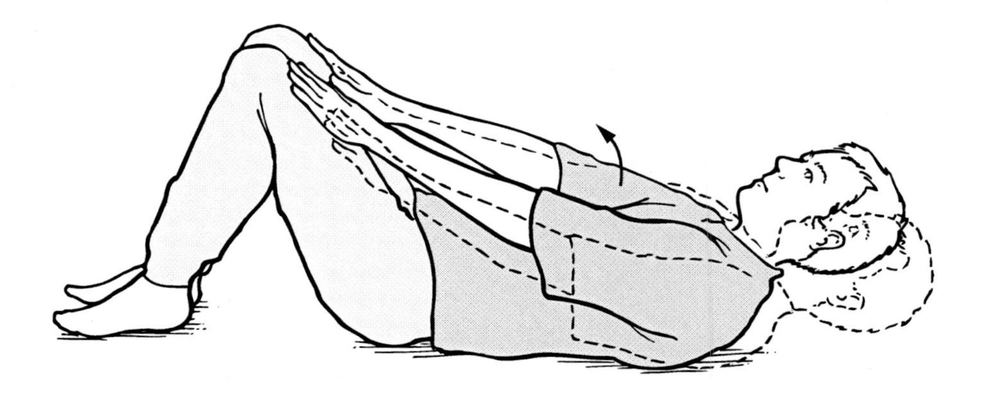

*Figure 58 Abdominals and pelvic tuck*

## OPPOSITE ARM/LEG LIFT

**Easy version:**

1. In the crawling position, lift one leg to the horizontal keeping elbows straight.
2. Try not to let your body swing over the supporting knee: keep it in the middle.
3. Hold for 15 seconds.
4. Repeat on alternate sides four times.

*Figure 59a Opposite arm/leg lift*

**Harder version:**

1. In the crawling position, lift opposite arm and leg to horizontal position.
2. Try not to let your body swing over the supporting knee: keep it in the middle.
3. Hold for 15 seconds.
4. Repeat on alternate sides four times.

*Figure 59b Opposite arm/leg lift*

## LUMBAR SIDEBENDING

1. Lie flat on your back, knees straight, arms by your sides.
2. Pull one leg up at the hip to shorten the leg.
3. Hold for 2 seconds.
4. Relax and repeat with the other leg.
5. Repeat on alternate sides ten times.

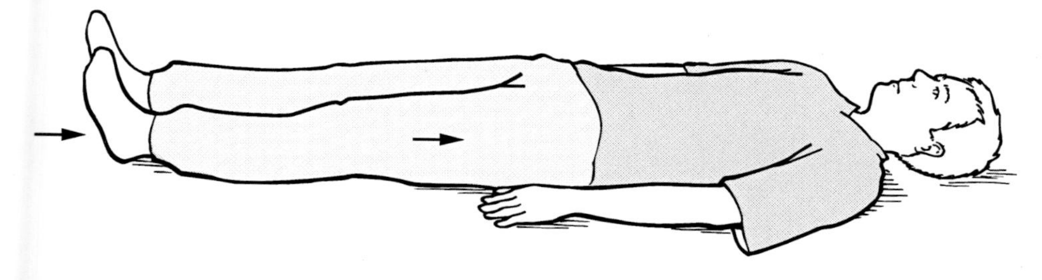

*Figure 60 Lumbar sidebending*

## ARM/LEG STRENGTH STRETCH

1 Lie face down with two pillows under your stomach, arms above your head.
2 Lift your opposite arm and leg approximately 20cm off the floor and stretch the two apart.
3 Hold this for 10 seconds.
4 Repeat on alternate sides four times.

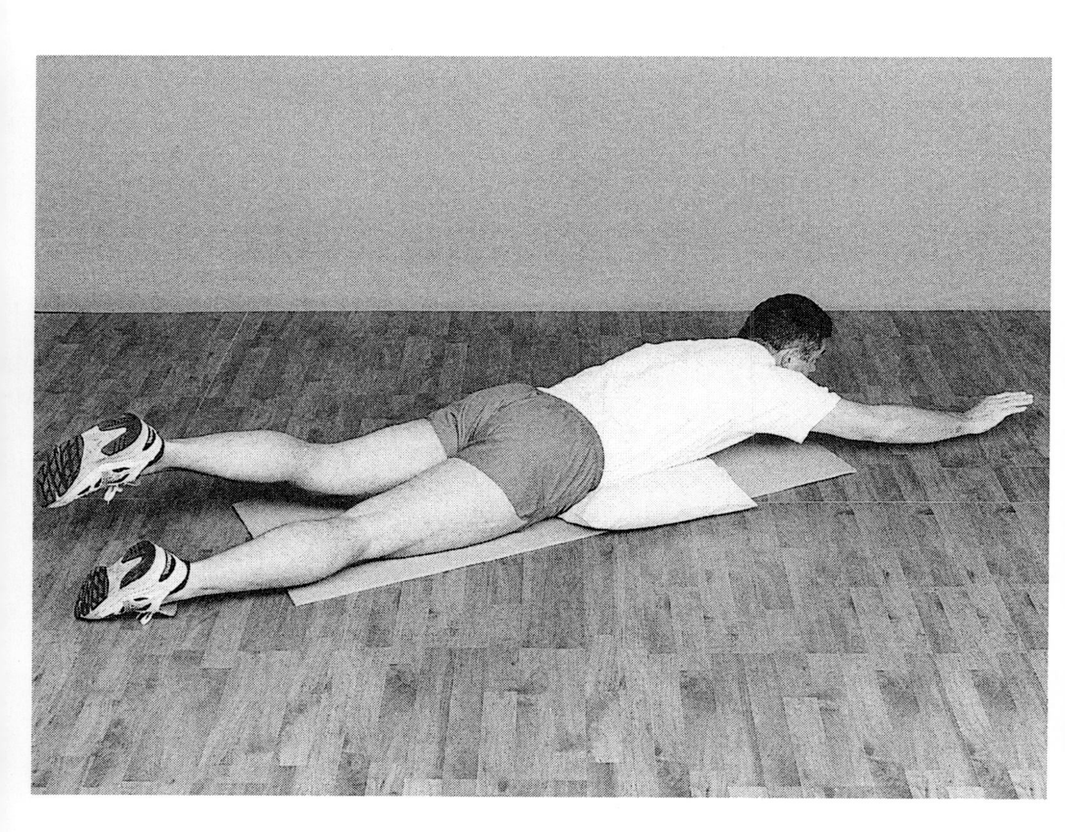

*Figure 61 Arm/leg strength stretch*

## PRONE EXTENSIONS

1. Lean your upper trunk over a table/bench/kitchen bar unit holding onto it. Use a cushion if necessary to soften the edge, which should be where your thighs meet your trunk.
2. Lift your straight legs up to the horizontal and hold for half a second.
3. Lower your legs back down to touch the floor with your toes.
4. Do about one every 2–3 seconds – no fast or jerky movements. Keep going until your lower back is tired, but not painful.

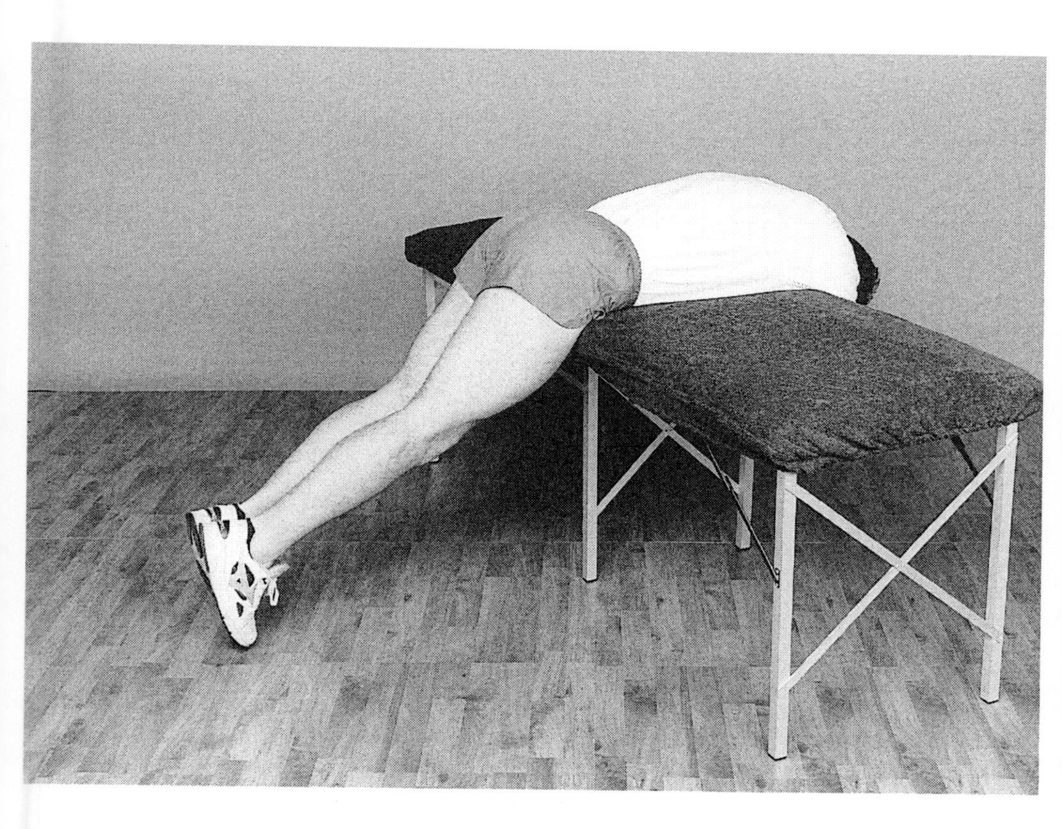

*Figure 62a Prone extensions*

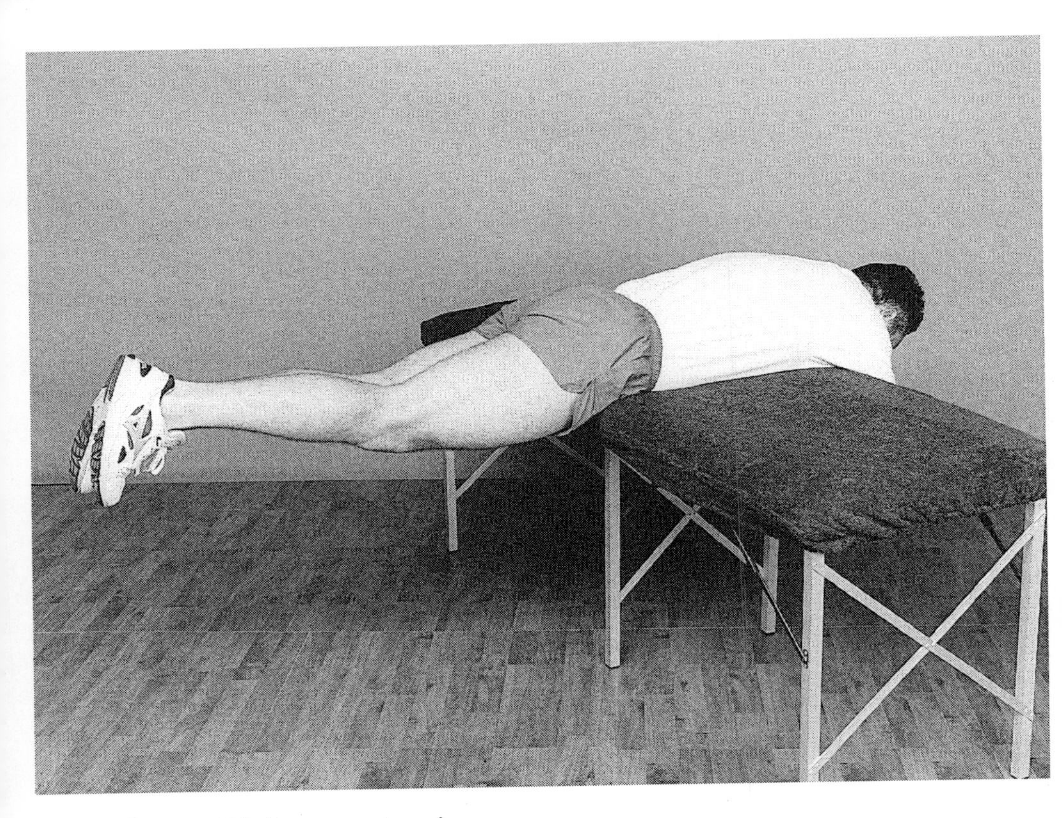

*Figure 62b Prone extensions*

**If you're generally fit and not overweight eventually you should be able to do 100 of these!**

## PRESS UPS

1. Lie face down with your palms on the floor, shoulder width apart, at shoulder level.
2. Keep your back and legs in a straight line.
3. Push up slowly and remember to straighten your elbows fully.
4. Lower yourself down until your elbows are at 90 degrees. Don't collapse fully onto the floor!
5. Repeat until your arms, chest or back are tired. Remember, no pain!

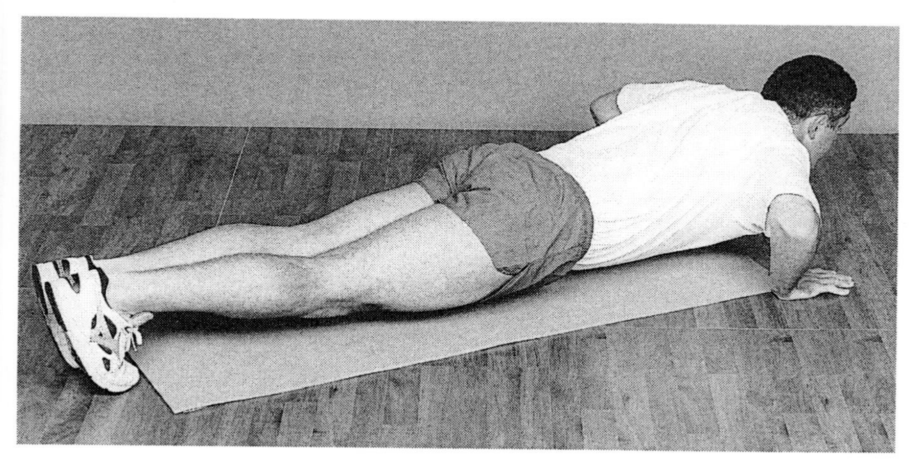

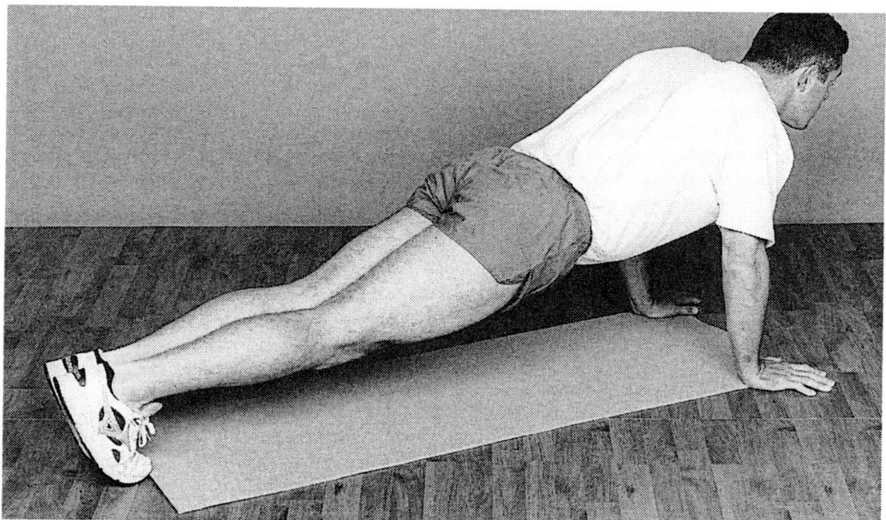

*Figure 63 Press ups*

## STANDING PELVIC TUCKS

1 Stand with your back to the wall and your knees fairly straight.
2 Contract your abdominal muscles so that your pelvis tucks underneath you and the curve in your lumbar spine flattens.
3 Hold for 3 seconds.
4 Repeat 10–20 times.

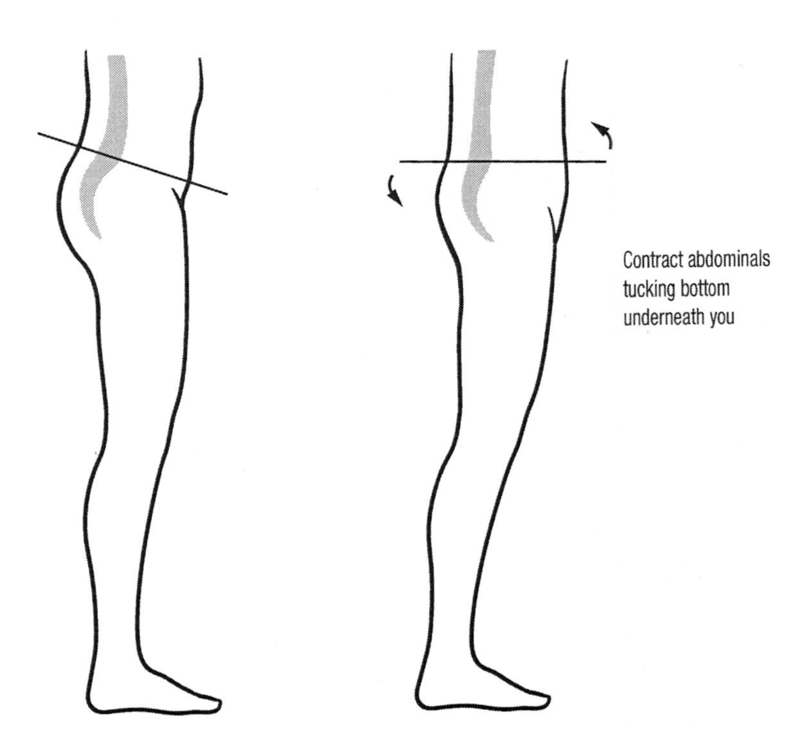


*Figure 64 Standing pelvic tucks*

## Planning Your Exercise Programme

How important to you is it that you get better? If it's very important then you must make your exercise programme a priority. Remember there are two main aspects your exercise programme must work on:

- **Flexibility**
- **Endurance**

So, you must select from the above exercises those that will improve both of these aspects. To start with we suggest trying all the exercises nice and gently, just to get a feel for them and what effort they require. Just because an exercise may be easy does not mean it's not worth doing.

Having tried the different exercises, work out a programme of exercise that will make you work reasonably hard and yet not make your back really sore. We suggest you aim for the following:

- **One exercise session combining endurance and stretching exercises each day.**
- **Two other exercise sessions each day with only stretching exercises.**
- **Swimming/walking/cycling three times per week.**

Your main exercise session of the day (one that includes endurance and stretching exercises) should take at least 15 minutes.

## THE BEGINNER'S EXERCISE PROGRAMME

- Gluteal stretch: one stretch each side.
- Abdominals: aim for 30 repetitions.
- Opposite arm/leg raise: aim for four repetitions, alternate sides.
- Lumbar sidebending: aim for ten repetitions each side, alternating.
- Gluteal stretch: do three each side, alternating.
- Hamstring stretch: do three each side, alternating.
- Crucifix: do two each side, alternating.
- Lumbar flexion: rock for 30 seconds.

## THE ADVANCED EXERCISE PROGRAMME

- Prone extensions: aim for 70 repetitions, but you should (when your back is in top form) be able to do 100 repetitions without stopping.
- Abdominals: 40 repetitions.
- Press ups: do 20–50 repetitions, depending on your capability.
- Prone extensions: aim for 40 repetitions, but you should (when your back is in top form) be able to do 100 repetitions without stopping.
- Abdominals: do 40 repetitions.
- Gluteal stretch: do three repetitions each side, alternating.
- Hamstring stretch: do three repetitions each side, alternating.
- Crucifix: do two repetitions each side, alternating.
- Lumbar extension: rest on elbows for 30 seconds.
- Psoas stretch: do three each side, alternating.
- Lumbar flexion: rock for 30 seconds.

Relax for a minute after this in whatever position you find restful. The number of repetitions given above is only a guide – do not over do it!

## THE EXERCISE PROGRAMME FOR THE WORKPLACE

The above programmes of exercises are preferred. However, if it's difficult for you to find somewhere to lie down, the exercise routine described below may be more suitable. When at home, make an effort to do one of the above exercise routines, as the one below does not include any strengthening exercises.

- **Standing gluteal stretch: three repetitions each side, alternating.**
- **Standing hamstring stretch: three repetitions each side, alternating.**
- **Calf stretch: three repetitions each side, alternating.**
- **Quadriceps stretch: three repetitions each side, alternating.**
- **Standing lumbar extensions: ten repetitions.**
- **Standing pelvic tucks: ten repetitions.**
- **Sitting rotations: five repetitions, alternating.**

# Bad Bending and Good Bending

- The Importance of Bending 'Properly'
- Bad Bending
- Good Bending

## The Importance of Bending 'Properly'

When you bend forwards you increase the strain on your back considerably. Bending to 30 degrees triples the forces on the discs in your lower back! If your back (and your health) is not in top form (or is simply tired) then you are at risk of overloading your back and straining it.

## Bad Bending

Bad bending depends on how fit and strong your back is. If you're in good health, bending straight forwards from the waist should not cause you any problems. However, most chronic back pain sufferers should be wary of this (*see figure* 65), and particularly wary of bending and twisting at the same time.

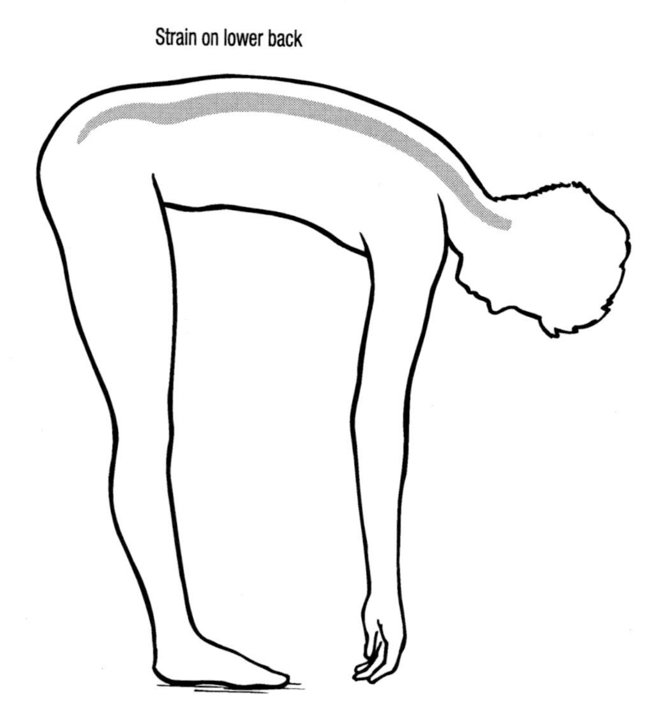


***Figure 65 Bending from the waist***

## Good Bending

You need to bend in a way that minimizes the strain on your back (*see figure* 66).

By bending from the knees, you keep your back straight, which means you are less likely to hurt something in your lower back. By bending forwards on one leg, with the other leg coming up behind you, your back is kept fairly straight. The leg behind you acts as a counter balance to the weight of your trunk going forwards – this tactic should not be used for picking up anything heavier than a box of tissues!

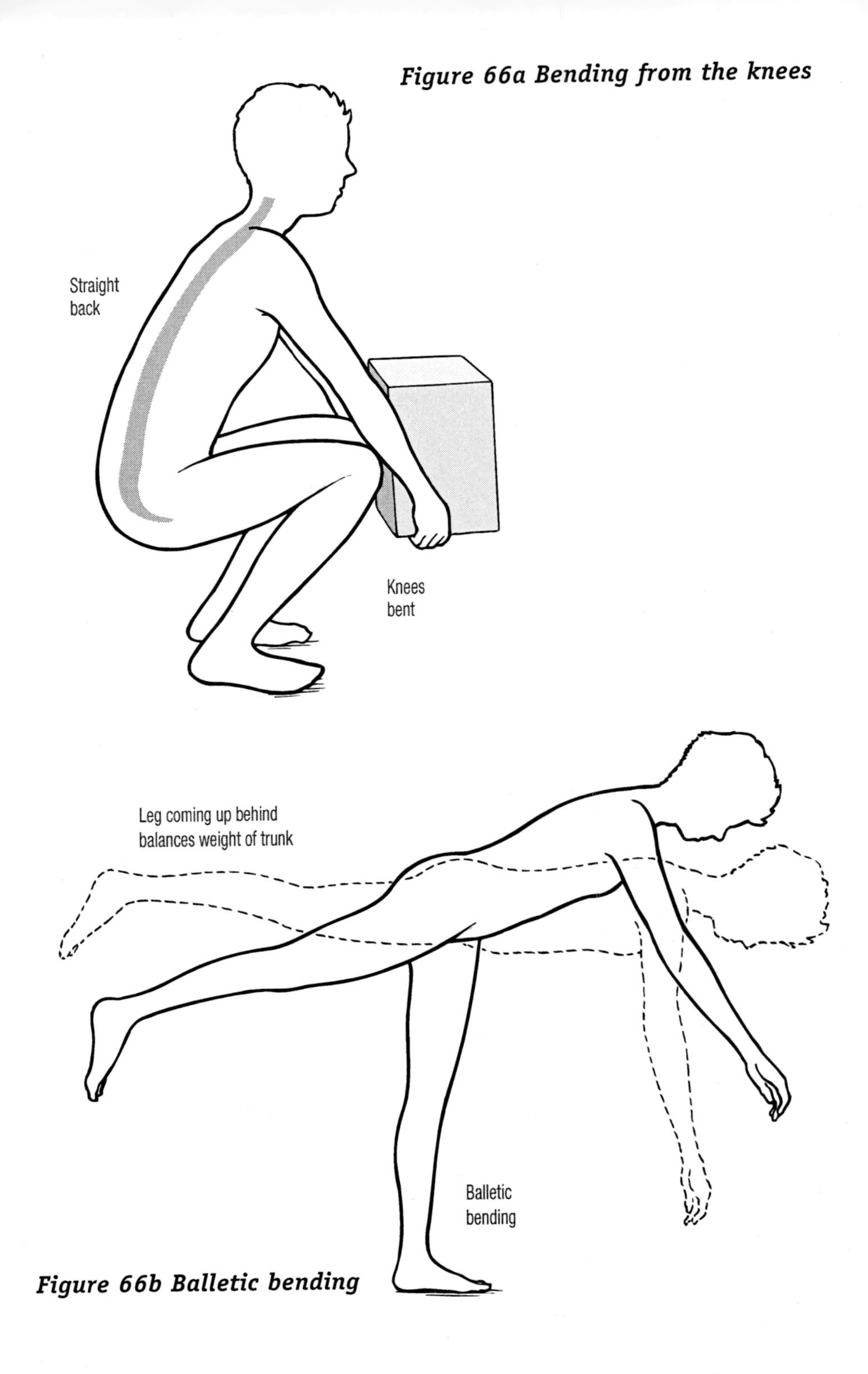


*Figure 66a Bending from the knees*

*Figure 66b Balletic bending*

# Bad Lifting and Good Lifting

- Bad Lifting
- Good Lifting and Carrying
- Handbags

## Bad Lifting

When you lift any object there is usually an element of bending involved. So refer first to the section above on bending. Always bend from the knees if lifting anything that cannot be easily lifted in one hand (*see figure* 66).

***Figure 67 Bad lifting: the spine is bent and the load is at arms' length***

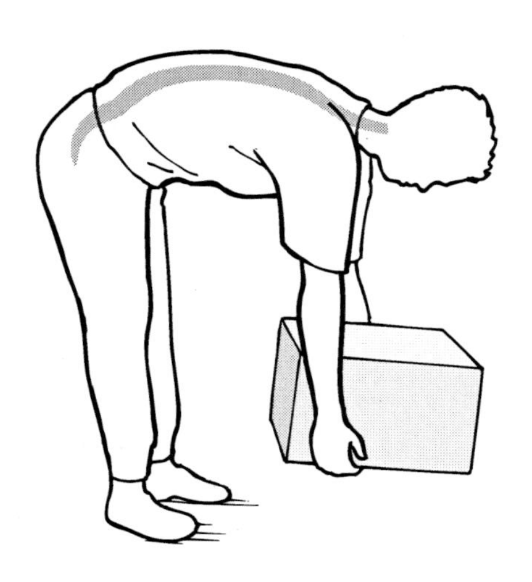

When lifting and carrying objects you increase the load on your lower back. The further the load is from your centre of gravity, the greater the strain on you: the further you hold the object from you, the greater the effort you need to make. Try holding a heavy bag at arms' length (but don't hurt your back), and then close in to your body – which is easier?

## Good Lifting and Carrying

As you can see above, good lifting means bending your knees and keeping the load in close to your body (*see figure* 68). **If confronted by a heavy weight, always try and get help to lighten the load.**

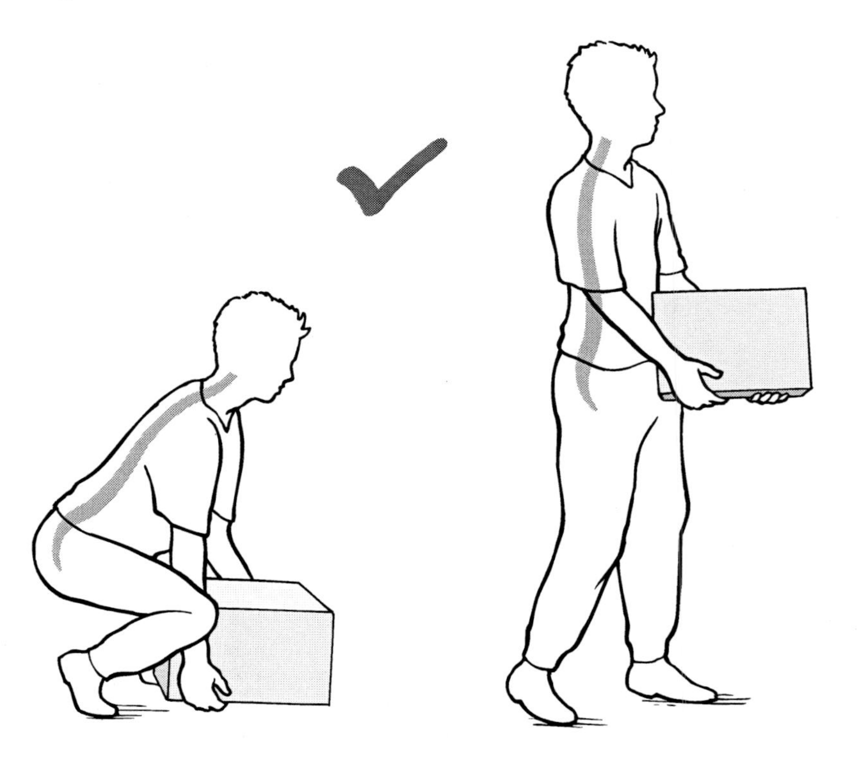

***Figure 68 The correct way to lift***

- **Prepare for the lift – do some stretch and warm up exercises – would you rather look silly now or be in pain for weeks?**
- **Bend your knees.**
- **Get close to the object to be lifted.**
- **Be sure you have a firm grip that will not slip.**
- **Take the strain.**
- **Slowly straighten your knees, holding the object close in to you.**
- **Do not twist on planted feet. Turn your whole body around from your feet if you need to turn.**
- **Lower the object by bending your knees again.**

If you are lifting with someone else, always make sure beforehand that you have agreed how and when you're going to lift. When carrying objects, such as shopping bags, at your sides, try and spread the load evenly between the two sides. Again, keep the load close in to you. Do not carry more than you need to.

## Handbags

Any bag – no matter how light it seems – if carried frequently on one shoulder, will gradually create uneven muscle tensions which may lead to pain. Try and swap shoulders or wear the bag across yourself – this spreads the load much more evenly.

# Other Useful Advice

- **Getting In and Out of the Car**
- **Getting Things Out of the Car Boot**
- **Standing at Kitchen Units/Sink**
- **Washing Your Hair in the Sink**
- **Tying Shoelaces and Putting on Socks**
- **Standing Up From a Chair**
- **Sitting Down on a Chair**
- **Reaching for Things on the Floor When Sitting**

## Getting In and Out of the Car

This is something that many of us do every day. As such it's something worth paying attention to. If you jump into your car as if you're taking part in a high speed pursuit of a runaway criminal then you're putting yourself at great risk of injury, and will certainly aggravate your back if you're already in pain.

If you have recently experienced low back pain then try the following:

1. **Turn your back to the car.**
2. **Lower yourself down gently onto the seat.**
3. **Move your bottom around slowly on the seat so that you're facing forwards.**
4. **Lift the inner leg in before the outer one.**

*Figure 69 Getting into a car*

You should get out by reversing this process, one leg at a time. If you are not suffering from back pain, and wish to stay this way then follow the above guidelines, missing out the first step.

## Getting Things Out of the Car Boot

*See section on lifting page 127.*

- ***Do not*** **try and lift things from deep in the boot (*see figure* 70).**
- **Pull the items right to the lip of the boot.**
- **Get a good grip and lift the item close in to your body.**
- **Get help if it's really heavy.**
- ***Do not*** **carry more than you need to!**

***Figure 70 How* not *to unload your boot***

## Standing at Kitchen Units/Sink

Many activities, including peeling potatoes, brushing your teeth and shaving, involve slight bending forwards, reaching with the hands. Rather than stand with your feet side by side, stand with one foot in front of the other and bend from the knees. Stoop forwards by bending from the hips, not from the waist. Bend your knees also. It's very difficult to bend both your knees at the kitchen sink if your feet are side by side, because your knees bang against the undersink cupboard doors, so put one leg behind the other.

## Washing Your Hair in the Sink

Bending your head forwards into the sink or kneeling with your head over the bath is a perfect way to aggravate your back, so take a shower instead!

## Tying Shoelaces and Putting On Socks

- **You can do this sitting down, crossing one ankle over the other knee to reach your foot.**
- **You can do it standing up, balancing on one foot.**
- **You can do it standing up with one foot resting on a chair – bend your supporting knee to come down, not your back.**
- **You can get someone else to do it!**

Use a shoe horn to avoid straining.

## Standing Up From a Chair

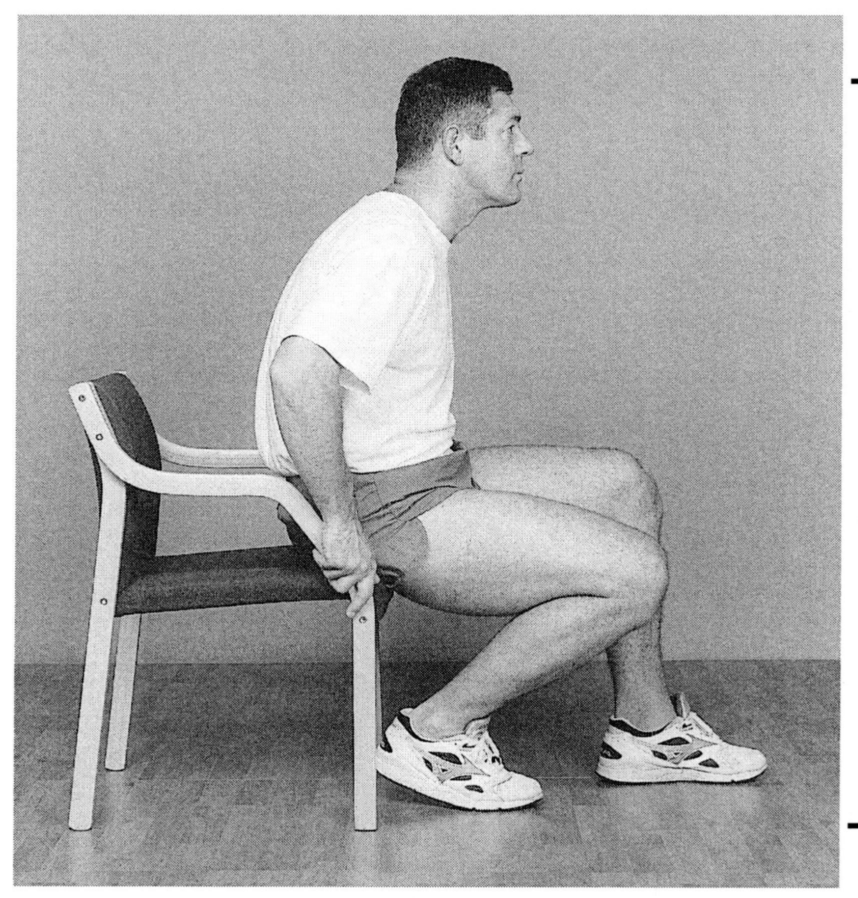

*Figure 71 How to stand up from a chair*

1 Move your bottom to the front edge of the chair.
2 Put one foot in front of the other.
3 Bend forwards from the hips (not the lower back).
4 Let the momentum of this forward movement carry you forwards and up.

## Sitting Down on a Chair

1 Turn your back to the chair.
2 Relax the hips and back so that your bottom moves down onto the chair.

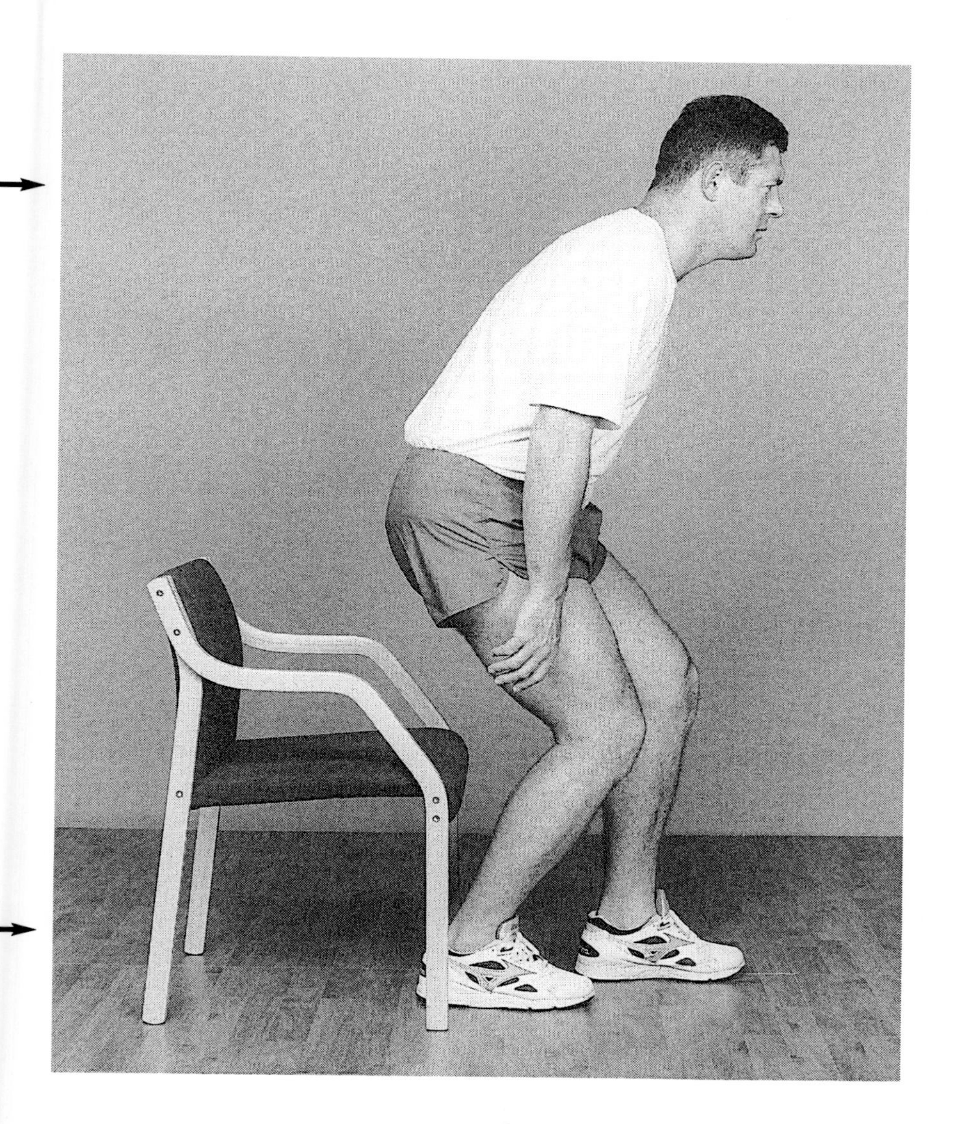

3 **Shuffle your bottom back on the seat.**
4 ***Never fall back into a chair!***

## Reaching for Things on the Floor When Sitting

Never bend down forwards or sideways when you are sitting: this puts a huge strain on your lower back. It is better to get up then squat down again to pick something up.

# Back Pain in Sports People

Back pain in sports people is dealt with pretty much in the same way as back pain in a non-sporting person: Use it or Lose it but don't ever Abuse it! If you are generally fit you should cope with injury better and recover faster, unless your sport or training is contributing to your back problems.

To speed up your recovery it is essential for you to consult a good chiropractor, osteopath or physiotherapist, preferably one with an interest in sports. This will help to establish the exact diagnosis and whether there is something you are doing to contribute to the problem – through your sport or otherwise. Your training can be modified to work around this problem.

Although it's terrible to be the bringer of bad news, it may be that your therapist advises you to take a break from your training or sport. He/she is doing this for your own good in the long run. If you do not allow an injury to recover fully now it may never resolve completely and could hamper your performance forever. If you're not satisfied with the diagnosis and management plan, then seek a second opinion. Follow your therapist's advice closely; do not make the mistake of doing more of a given exercise than prescribed, on the basis that if three of something is good for you then 30 of it must be ten times better!

In terms of the diagnosis of your problem – this is no different to any other person: it may be called a 'sports injury' but this merely means you did it while participating in sport. Your anatomy is the same as someone who does not participate in sport: you have exactly the same tissues. It is only the management of your problem and you that may be different to that of a non-sporting person. Each person's management is slightly different, because we are all different to one another, and all demand different things of our bodies.

In sport there are some very obvious ways to damage your back:

- **Fast bowling in cricket – the left side of the spine is under great pressure in a right armed bowler as he uses this side to decelerate rapidly.**
- **Golf can lead to over-rotation of the spine.**
- **Squash and badminton require fast twisting, turning and bending movements.**
- **Horse riding commonly results in chronic low back strain.**
- **Weight training increases the load on your lower back considerably.**
- **Physical contact in sport (e.g. rugby) adds to the risk of damaging your back.**

To guard against the hazards involved in these activities your training must take the risk of back injury into account. The lower back is often an area that is ignored in training regimes – perhaps because you don't often see your own back!

In sport you are asking more of your body than in most everyday activities, so you must train for this appropriately. This means working on your flexibility and endurance and, for sports such as wrestling, judo and rugby, your sheer strength also. The exercises in this book can be used to achieve greater flexibility and endurance, although for sheer strength you may need to visit a gym for weight training advice. The prone extension exercise (*page 117*) can be done with ankle weights on to increase the load on your lower back.

Sports people should be more aware that in preparing for a particular sport you need to pay attention to total fitness. Any weakness will be exposed – a boxer with a big right hook still needs very good abdominal muscles to absorb the punches he will undoubtedly receive.

# Back Pain in Pregnancy

This is a common problem – not surprisingly! Think about it – over a matter of months a woman gains roughly 2 stone in weight, most of it around the belly; her posture changes dramatically and her ligaments start to slacken in order to prepare for birth.

The change in posture alone can result in stresses being passed to tissues such as muscles and ligaments, which are not used to this amount of strain. Consequently, these tissues protest – pain! In the last few months a woman's pelvis is preparing for the birth process: the ligaments slacken and allow more movement in the sacro-iliac joints and at the pubic symphysis. This makes these joints more prone to being strained, which can be very sore, making getting around very difficult. The best advice in this situation is to get off to see a chiropractor, osteopath or physiotherapist, who, apart from easing the situation for you, will give you advice on the birthing process as well if you ask for it!

Getting comfortable in bed can be quite difficult. Generally you will not be able to lie on your front. Lying on your back could be very uncomfortable due to the weight of the baby lying on your bladder and other abdominal contents. So, most women end up lying on their sides. In this position, you may find it helpful to have a pillow between your knees to keep the pelvis level, and a thin pillow underneath your belly to stop yourself from rolling forwards with the weight of the baby.

The golden rule holds true for pregnant women as well – Use it or Lose it but don't ever Abuse it! You should continue to take exercise within the limits of your discomfort – if it hurts don't do it! On the other hand, if you just sit or lie around waiting for your baby to appear, your muscles will waste and your joints seize up making delivery that much harder, and you will not recover from the birth as quickly. So, be sensible – don't tire yourself out, but don't tire your chair out either. Again, if in doubt, speak to your chiropractor, osteopath or physiotherapist.

There is often controversy over how much you should work your abdominal muscles. If your abdominal muscles are well exercised during pregnancy they should not tire as quickly during delivery as they would if you do no exercise at all. Very few women suffer from over development of their abdominal muscles! Remember that they will have a lot of work to do during delivery – almost certainly more than ever before, so you should prepare for this. Do abdominal strengthening exercises every day. And remember to do your pelvic floor exercises on the toilet (there's no reason why these can't be done at other times as well).

Sometimes you will get back pain because the baby is lying awkwardly and pushing on something, creating pain. You may also get severe 'sciatica' if the baby lies on your sciatic nerve – try lying on the other side to encourage the baby to move over! Pain and/or pins and needles down the front of the thigh may be caused by the baby lying very far forward in the pelvis, stretching your femoral nerve – go and see a chiropractor, osteopath or physiotherapist.

Do not make the mistake of believing that all pain in your lower back, pelvis or legs is due to the baby pushing on something. If the pain is not relieved by changing position and getting the baby to shift around then consult a chiropractor, osteopath or physiotherapist.

N.B. First time parents are particularly at risk of low back pain as they are suddenly doing more bending, lifting and carrying. The ideal would be to go into training for parenthood. Perhaps emotionally as well as physically!

# Tests, Investigations and Surgery

- X-rays
- CAT Scans
- MRI Scans
- Blood Tests
- Surgery
- Chemonucleolysis

Sometimes you may be advised that the best thing for your back problem is surgery. This is a big topic and should be discussed with your surgeon and also your chiropractor, osteopath or physiotherapist, to get as balanced a view as possible. There are various surgical procedures for different spinal problems, but the most common one is an operation to relieve pressure on a spinal nerve, caused by a disc pushing on it. A brief description of this surgery is given here, but first we describe the different tests and investigations that may be performed and their merits.

## X-rays

X-rays are a vastly over-used investigation for lower back pain. They give a picture of the bones and any other dense (compact) tissue (like kidney stones). Often the x-ray may show a problem which is not causing you any pain. That is, you may have lots of degenerative changes (spondylosis) on your x-ray but no pain at all. Or you may have no sign of anything wrong on your x-ray, but lots of severe pain. This is the problem with x-rays – they can only show you the state of the bones and the joints where the bones meet. Your muscles, ligaments, tendons, discs and other soft tissues will not be shown on an x-ray.

The discs are shown as spaces in between the bones. If one of these spaces is thinner than expected it may be thought that this disc has been flattened, but this does not necessarily mean a prolapse.

## CAT (or CT) Scanning

CT (Computed Tomography) involves x-rays being fired at the body from different angles, giving a picture of any level or area chosen – like a slice of the body. It is more detailed than an x-ray and will show the softer tissues as well as the bones.

## MRI or Magnetic Resonance Imaging

For this test you have to lie very still in a large tube which exerts a strong magnetic field on your body. This procedure produces high quality pictures of any part of your body. People who have heart pacemakers or any metalwork inside their bodies (surgical plates or screws) may not be able to undergo this investigation. People who are claustrophobic (frightened of enclosed spaces) may not cope with this procedure as you have to lie very still inside this tube for half an hour. This is now the investigation most doctors will want to undertake if contemplating surgery. However, the MRI machines are very expensive and so in short supply within the NHS. Consequently there can be quite a waiting list.

## Blood Tests

A blood sample may be taken to send off for more general tests. You may be tested for inflammatory joint disease, anaemia or other problems.

## Surgery

Surgery for suspected disc problems will usually only be undertaken if there is:

- **Disc prolapse shown on MRI or CAT scan.**

AND one of the following:

- **No improvement in symptoms (how you feel) and signs.**
- **Increase in neurological deficit – numbness or muscle weakness.**
- **Bladder or bowel involvement – difficulty with urination or defecation.**
- **Unbearable pain.**

### (PARTIAL) DISCECTOMY

This means removal ('ectomy') of the disc or that part of it (partial) that is causing the problem. Part of the bone just behind the nerve and the ligament attached to it are frequently removed (laminectomy). Any disc material not forming part of the disc itself (prolapsed material) is removed from around this area also. This process relieves the pressure on the nerve from the surrounding tissues (*see figure* 72).

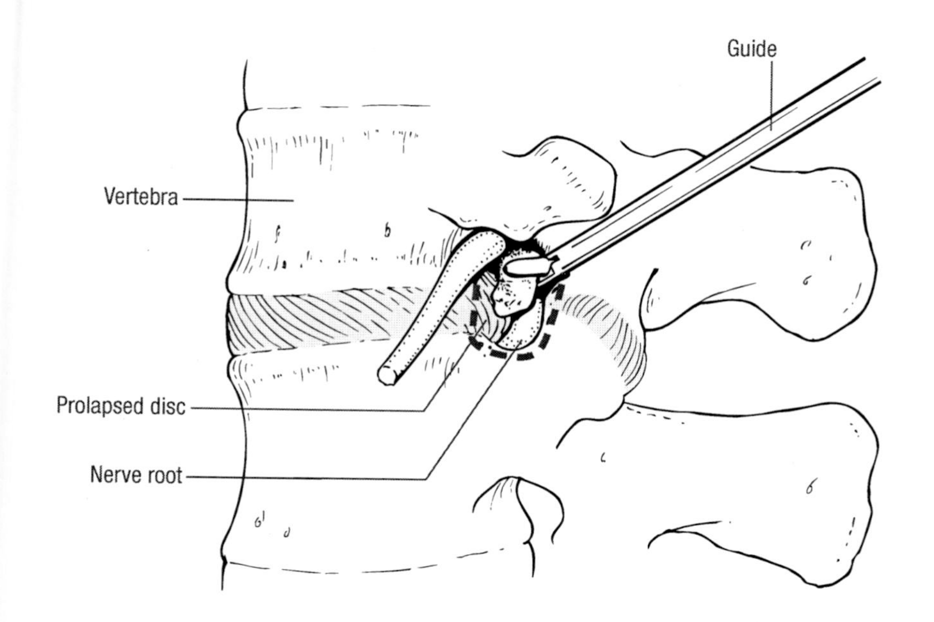


***Figure 72 Removal of disc material and laminectomy***

Microdiscectomy can be carried out through a very small skin cut allowing the surgeon to pass thin wires (containing a fibreoptic wire) into the back. This gives the surgeon a television view of the problem area without having to make such a big cut. This operation generally involves much less trauma to the surrounding tissues, but the jury is still out on whether it is a better option: because the surgeon has a less complete view it is perhaps more difficult to perform. Don't be shy – ask your surgeon how many he/she has done.

## Chemonucleolysis – Chymopapaine Injection

This involves the injection of a chemical which breaks down the disc material around the nerve root, and in some hospitals it is preferred to surgery. It has much the same success rate as surgery but works best for those who have only had a disc problem for a short time.

You should feel happy that you have discussed the chances of success with all concerned – particularly the surgeon – before undergoing surgery. There are no guarantees of success, but the results can be fantastic and immediate for some lucky patients.

These procedures – surgery and injection – should be seen as part of the overall management of your back problem, not as a complete solution. You should still follow the advice in this book, but do so in conjunction with the advice from your surgeon and chiropractor, osteopath or physiotherapist.

# Painkilling Drugs

- Pain Relievers Only
- Non-steroidal Anti-inflammatories
- Morphine-related Pain Killers For Severe Pain
- Common Side Effects
- TENS

## Pain Relievers Only

For pain that worsens with use during the day and is generally better in the morning.

- **Paracetamol: available over the counter at your pharmacy.**
- **Dihydrocodeine (DF118): available on prescription from your doctor.**
- **Dextropropoxyphyene & paracetamol (Coproxamol/Distalgesic/DGs): available from your doctor.**

## Non-steroidal Anti-inflammatories

For pain and stiffness at rest, particularly on awakening in the morning, relieved a little by movement and aggravated if you do too much.

- **Aspirin: available over the counter.**
- **Ibuprofen (Brufen): available over the counter or in a stronger form on prescription from your doctor.**
- **Naproxen (Naprosyn): available from your doctor.**
- **Ketoprofen (Orudis): available from your doctor.**

- **Diclofenac (Voltarol): available from your doctor.**
- **Azapropazone (Rheumox*): available from your doctor.***
- **Piroxicam (Feldene): available from your doctor.**
- **Indomethacin (Indocid): available from your doctor.**

## Morphine-related Painkillers for Severe Pain

- **Morphine or pethidine: only available from your doctor, and often given by injection.**

Some of these painkillers may be given in suppository form (up your bottom!) as this releases the drug more slowly. This is often offered if you tend to suffer from an irritable stomach as some of the drugs above can be quite harsh on the lining of your stomach. Your body will respond in its own way to these drugs, so just because something worked miracles for your friend's pain does not mean it will do the same for yours.

You should take the pills regularly throughout the day if the pain is steady; if the pain peaks at certain times try and take the pills half to one hour before this time. But always stick to the dosage prescribed by your doctor.

## Common Side Effects

| | |
|---|---|
| Non-steroidal anti-inflammatories* | Indigestion/stomach ulceration/bleeding* |
| The codeine-based painkillers | Constipation, dizziness |
| Morphine-related painkillers | Sleepiness, nausea |

*Non-steroidal anti-inflammatories frequently cause mild nausea and indigestion – this is a sign that you should speak to your doctor about the advisability of continuing with these drugs – you don't want a stomach ulcer as well!

## Transcutaneous Electrical Nerve Stimulation (TENS)

TENS consists of a small battery-powered pack (about the size of a cigarette packet) with two leads and two rubber pads. The rubber pads are stuck to your skin: usually one pad is over the spine and one over the site of your pain, with no more than 8 inches between them.

An electrical current passes between the two pads, affecting the transmission of impulses along your nerves. This electrical current causes a fine prickling sensation – it is not unpleasant. The idea is that this prickling masks the pain. TENS is used commonly by women in labour, and has been shown to relieve back pain. It is NOT a cure, but like painkillers it masks the pain. If this helps you to get moving then it serves a useful purpose; but do not rely on it to make you better. Just like taking painkillers, this should only be resorted to if it contributes to you being able to do more to help yourself. Do not think of it as the answer to all your troubles! Read the instructions that come with the pack – they will help you to use it properly.

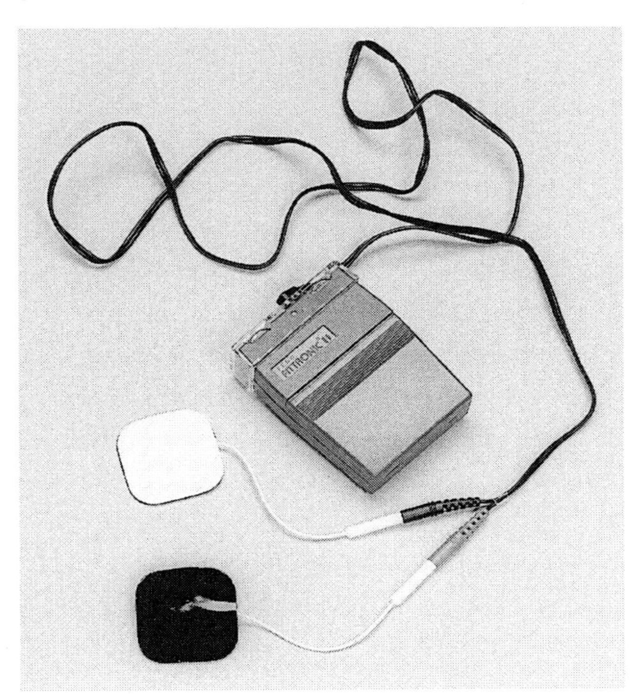

# Other Sources of Help

- **Acupuncture**
- **Alexander Technique**
- **Massage**
- **Aromatherapy**
- **Occupational Therapy**

There are a host of other potential sources of help for those with low back pain. The most commonly used are briefly described here. As with finding a chiropractor, osteopath or physiotherapist it is generally better to get a personal recommendation.

## Acupuncture

Acupuncture is an ancient Chinese medicinal art. Other methods used by the Chinese include herbalism and massage. Acupuncture has been practised in China for thousands of years, while our Western system of modern medicine is only a couple of hundred years old. Acupuncture is a truly 'holistic' approach to health care: the acupuncturist treats the individual and not the symptoms that the individual complains of. It aims to boost the patient's health in every way so that the patient can use his/her own coping mechanisms to resolve any problem – cough, cold, sore back etc. Unlike other systems of medicine, acupuncture diagnoses the person, not the ailment. The acupuncturist may diagnose a long-standing weakness in the patient, and believes any current ailment is a result of this problem. So treatment is aimed at this weakness and not generally at the current problem. This contrasts significantly with Western medicine and its specializations, where a lot of effort goes into establishing the nature of the disease process and treatment is aimed at this. For example, in dealing with someone with breathing difficulties the Western doctor may diagnose asthma and prescribe drugs to ease the breathing difficulties, whereas the acupuncturist may diagnose poor 'lung energy' and treat this. They are simply different approaches neither being 'right' or 'wrong'.

Acupuncture recognizes the 'energy' in people, called 'Qi' (pronounced 'Chee'), and attempts to regulate this energy by inserting needles at various points around the body. The needles used are very fine, and most acupuncturists use disposable needles – those that do not will ensure that the needles are fully sterilized between patients – if in doubt, then ask. It is likely that the acupuncturist will insert needles at points distant from your lower back – bear in mind that he/she is treating you and not just your back pain.

Some clinicians (doctors, physiotherapists, osteopaths) do courses in acupuncture. I believe that if you are looking to try acupuncture you should consult an out and out acupuncturist, not someone who has done a 3 month course in acupuncture. Most acupuncturists study for at least 3 years. The address of the British Acupuncture Council is given in the Appendix.

Consultations usually cost between £20 and £50, depending on the experience of the practitioner and the duration of the session.

## Alexander Technique

This is a system developed by F.M. Alexander. It concentrates on the importance of balanced posture and movement. From childhood we learn how to move – lying, sitting, crawling, standing, walking, running – by watching others and experimenting and developing our own 'neural pathways'. Add to this sitting at desks, working computers, driving – all the things that we do without thinking. Throughout life we keep modifying these neural pathways, influenced by accidents, injuries and environmental stress. Imperceptibly these factors lead to 'poor' posture and unbalanced movement patterns resulting in aches and pains that at first seem to have come from nowhere, or inconsistent sleep patterns, or the feeling of never keeping up. The Alexander Technique is a gentle, non-invasive process of re-educating the body's current neural pathways to regain flexibility in posture and movement.

The Alexander Technique teacher guides you through the process of changing your postures – sitting, standing and lying. The process is individual to you and is a very active one for you. It is not something that is done to you – you take part and actively learn from the teacher how to help your body to function better and so decrease the stresses on it and you.

Lessons usually cost between £15 and £30. Some practitioners run group classes at a lower cost.

## Massage

Massage is perhaps the oldest form of caring known to man. It is the most natural thing to do when something hurts: to rub it. This basic instinct has been developed in different cultures in different ways: in the Far East there is shiatsu, in Europe there are various forms of massage, including sports massage, Swedish massage and remedial massage. Many of these use similar techniques. Massage is the application of rubbing, squeezing, pressing and kneading techniques to bring about changes in the body. These techniques generally improve circulation, wash away waste products, loosen muscle tissues and help to relax people. This will often help to relieve aches in the lower back and if yours is primarily a muscular problem, massage may help to resolve the pain entirely.

However, if there is a mechanical imbalance due to injury or ongoing postural strains, massage is unlikely to get to the root of the problem. It may feel easier, but the pain will soon return.

Sessions usually cost between £20 and £40, depending on the experience of the practitioner and the duration of the session.

## Aromatherapy

Aromatherapy has become very popular over the last 10 years. Essential oils (extracted from plants) are believed to have certain properties which can be used therapeutically. There are more than 50 different essential oils, each having its own action on you and its own aroma!

These oils can be used in your bath, burnt in an oil burner or used in massage oils. If you wish to use the oils yourself you should take advice as they are potent substances and can burn the skin. Having an aromatherapy massage is a relaxing way to benefit from the powers of the different oils. You may prefer this to straight massage, though if it's massage you're after you should set more store in the abilities of the masseur than in the oils themselves.

Sessions usually cost between £25 and £40.

## Occupational Therapy

This is the science of applying knowledge of human body function to everyday activities. An occupational therapist will advise you specifically on how to do your daily activities in a way that minimizes the strain on your lower back (or any other bit that ails you). Occupational therapists are thin on the ground in the private sector – the vast majority working within the NHS with people who are severely disabled. However, their skills are much underused by back pain sufferers. Chiropractors, osteopaths and physiotherapists do give similar advice, but this is not their field of expertise, and so the advice given is probably less detailed.

Sessions usually cost between £25 and £50, depending on whether it takes place in consulting rooms or in your own home, the latter being more expensive.

# Recommended Reading

## Arthritis

*Exercise Beats Arthritis*, Sayce and Fraser, Thorsons

## Diet

*Eat Orgasmically and Still Lose weight*, Dr Deanna Jepson, Thorsons
*Let's Eat Right to Keep Fit*, Adelle Davis, Thorsons
*Weight Control*, Stephen Terrass, Thorsons
*The Zone*, Dr Barry Sears with Bill Lauren, Thorsons

## Osteoporosis

*The Osteoporosis Handbook*, Sydney Lou Bonnick, Taylor

## Yoga

*Principles of Yoga*, Sara Martin, Thorsons
*Yoga, Step By Step*, Cheryl Isaacson, Thorsons

# Appendix of Useful Organizations

**The Society of Teachers of the Alexander Technique**
1st Floor, Linton House
39-51 Highgate Road
London NW5 1RS
Tel: 0845 2307828
www.stat.org.uk

**British Osteopathic Association**
Langham House West
Mill Street
Luton
Bedfordshire
LU1 2NA
Tel: 01582 488455
www.osteopathy.org.uk

**The British Chiropractic Association**
Blagrave House
17 Blagrave Street
Reading
Berkshire
RG11QB
Tel: 0118 950 5950
www.chiropractic-uk.co.uk

**Chartered Society of Physiotherapy**
14 Bedford Row
London WC1R 4ED
Tel: 020 7306 6666
www.csp.org.uk

**BackCare – The charity for healthier backs**
16 Elmtree Road
Teddington
Middlesex
TW11 8ST
Tel: 0208 977 5474
www.backcare.org.uk

**British Acupuncture Council**
63 Jeddo Road
London
W12 9HQ
Tel: 0208 735 0400
www.acupuncture.org.uk

**Active X Osteopaths**
HQ: 24 & 26 West Port
Edinburgh
EH1 2JE
Tel: 0845 2601520